DATE DUE

GAYLORD | | | PRINTED IN U.S.A.

Cambridge Introductions to Literature

This series is designed to introduce students to key topics and authors. Accessible and lively, these introductions will also appeal to readers who want to broaden their understanding of the books and authors they enjoy.

- Ideal for students, teachers, and lecturers
- Concise, yet packed with essential information
- Key suggestions for further reading

Titles in this series:

The Cambridge Introduction to
Ezra Pound

IRA B. NADEL

CAMBRIDGE
UNIVERSITY PRESS

CAMBRIDGE UNIVERSITY PRESS
Cambridge, New York, Melbourne, Madrid, Cape Town, Singapore, São Paulo

Cambridge University Press
The Edinburgh Building, Cambridge CB2 8RU, UK

Published in the United States of America by Cambridge University Press, New York

www.cambridge.org
Information on this title: www.cambridge.org/9780521630696

First published 2007

Printed in the United Kingdom at the University Press, Cambridge

A catalogue record for this publication is available from the British Library

ISBN 978-0-521-85391-0 hardback
ISBN 978-0-521-63069-6 paperback

Contents

Preface

"My eyes are geared for the horizon," Ezra Pound wrote in 1938 (*Guide to Kulchur* 55). It's a telling remark suggesting the breadth and vision of his work, whether in poetry or prose. He thought big, although he argued for concrete details. He promoted large ideas but worked in pieces: his long opus, *The Cantos*, spanning some fifty-two years of construction. And he always urged, cajoled and pushed – some would say dumped – his ideas on the public. But he never said "enough" or gave up even when challenged by editors, fellow writers, or governments. This introduction to his life and work presents the many facets of Pound, who possessed a kind of binocular vision, able to look out to the horizon at the same time that he saw what was immediately in front of him. He knew that "language is made out of concrete things" but that a universal view was necessary. In one sense his program was simple – "if a man write six good lines he is immortal – isn't that worth trying for?" – but in another it was complex as he sought to become "*fra i maestri di color che sanno*," a phrase he expands as "master of those that cut apart, dissect and divide. Competent precursor of the card-index" (*SL* 49, 12; *Guide to Kulchur* 343).

Many have assisted with the "card indexes" of this project and I thank them, beginning with Ray Ryan, a patient, impatient, encouraging and, when necessary, an admonitory editor; Anne MacKenzie, support and guide, who knows the difference between clarity and confusion; Dara and Ryan, my children, who constantly encouraged me not only to "make it new," but make it short. And finally, those myriad Poundians who have charted the waters before me so that I may safely navigate between the often foggy shores.

Note on the text

The Cambridge Introduction to Ezra Pound provides a systematic approach to understanding the life, context, work and reception of this major modernist. Following a survey of Pound's life which took him from the American West to Philadelphia, Venice, London, Paris and Rapallo, and introduced him to figures like Yeats, Joyce and T. S. Eliot, is a section on "Context." This explores how Pound's efforts to "MAKE IT NEW" coincided with original work in music, art and literature occurring throughout Europe and North America, from 1909/10, – when Pound's *Personae*, Stravinsky's *Firebird* ballet and Henri Matisse's *The Dance* all appeared – to 1969, when Pound published the final volume of *The Cantos*, Samuel Beckett won the Nobel Prize for Literature and Claes Oldenburg completed his pop-art sculpture, *Lipstick (Ascending)*. The volume then traces the evolution of Pound's writing from his earliest attempts to the last Cantos. Prose, as well as poetry and translations, comprise this section which also shows how his aesthetic principles and involvement with such movements as Imagism and Vorticism relate to his writing. Pound's music and art criticism are also discussed. Attention to important individual texts like "Sestina Altaforte," "Homage to Sextus Propertius" and *Hugh Selwyn Mauberley* precede a discussion of Pound's life-time work, *The Cantos*. Broken down into units Pound himself designated – the "Malatesta Cantos," the "Chinese Cantos," the "Jefferson–Adam Cantos," "The Pisan Cantos" – is an analysis of the multiple structure, themes and language of *The Cantos*.

Pound's contested politics and economics are also addressed, noting the influences and detours they presented to his literary achievement. The controversial radio broadcasts he made between 1941 and 1943 from Fascist Italy are also discussed, as well as his search for heroes, which drew him to Confucius, Thomas Jefferson, John Adams and Mussolini. The critical reception of Pound and his wavering reputation conclude the book with an assessment of his contribution to, and redefinition of, modernism. A guide to further reading assists the student in pursuing the life and work of Pound. References to *The Cantos*, Pound's major work, are to Canto number and page number in the thirteenth printing by New Directions in 1995. The citation for "MAKE IT NEW" appears as LIII/265.

Abbreviations

ABCR	Ezra Pound, *ABC of Reading.* [1934.] New York: New Directions, 1960.
AV	W. B. Yeats, *A Vision.* New York: Macmillan, 1961.
CAD	Ezra Pound, *Classic Anthology as Defined by Confucius.* [1954.] London: Faber and Faber, 1974.
CC	*Confucius to Cummings, An Anthology of Poetry.* Ed. Ezra Pound and Marcella Spann. New York: New Directions, 1964.
CCEP	*The Cambridge Companion to Ezra Pound.* Ed. Ira B. Nadel. Cambridge: Cambridge University Press, 1999.
CEP	Ezra Pound, *Collected Early Poems of Ezra Pound.* Ed. Michael John King. New York: New Directions, 1976.
CRH	*Ezra Pound, The Critical Heritage.* Ed. Eric Homberger. London: Routledge & Kegan Paul, 1972.
END	H. D. [Hilda Doolittle], *End to Torment, A Memoir of Ezra Pound.* New York: New Directions, 1979.
EP/BC	Ezra Pound, *Ezra Pound and Senator Bronson Cutting: A Political Correspondence 1930–1935.* Ed. E. P. Walkiewicz and Hugh Witemeyer. Albuquerque, NM: University of New Mexico Press, 1995.
EPE	*The Ezra Pound Encyclopedia.* Ed. Demetres Tryphonopoulos and Stephen J. Adams. Westport, CT: Greenwood Press, 2005.
EPEW	Ezra Pound, *Early Writings, Poems and Prose.* Ed. Ira. B. Nadel. New York: Penguin, 2005.
EP/JL	Ezra Pound, *Ezra Pound and James Laughlin, Selected Letters.* Ed. David M. Gordon. New York: W. W. Norton, 1994.
EPM	[T. S. Eliot], "Ezra Pound: His Metric and Poetry," *to Criticize the Critic and Other Writings.* New York: Farrar Strauss Giroux, 1965. 162–82.
EPPT	Ezra Pound, *Poems and Translations.* Ed. Richard Sieburth. New York: Library of America, 2003.

EPS	Ezra Pound. *"Ezra Pound Speaking." Radio Speeches of World War II*. Ed. Leonard W. Doob. Westport, CT: Greenwood Press, 1978.
EPVA	*Ezra Pound and the Visual Arts*. Ed. Harriet Zinnes. New York: New Directions, 1980.
GAL	Donald Gallup, *Ezra Pound, A Bibliography*. 2nd edn. Charlottesville: University Press of Virginia, 1983.
GB	Ezra Pound, *Gaudier-Brzeska, A Memoir*. [1916.] New York: New Directions, 1970.
GK	Ezra Pound, *Guide to Kulchur*. [1938.] New York: New Directions, 1970.
Ind	Ezra Pound, *Indiscretions*, in *Pavannes & Divagations*. [1958.] New York: New Directions, 1974. 3–51.
J/M	Ezra Pound, *Jefferson and/or Mussolini*. London: Stanley Nott, 1935.
LC	Ezra and Dorothy Pound, *Letters in Captivity, 1945–46*. Ed. Omar Pound and Robert Spoo. New York: Oxford University Press, 1999.
LE	Ezra Pound, *Literary Essays*. Ed. T. S. Eliot. [1954.] New York: New Directions, 1968.
MAO	Ezra Pound, *Machine Art & Other Writings, The Lost Thought of the Italian Years*. Ed. Maria Luisa Ardizzone. Durham: Duke University Press, 1996.
PAT	William Carlos Williams, *Paterson*. New York: New Directions, 1958.
PE	Hugh Kenner, *The Pound Era*. Berkeley: University of California Press, 1971.
PEP	Hugh Kenner, *The Poetry of Ezra Pound*. [1951]. Lincoln: University of Nebraska Press, 1985.
P/F	Ezra Pound, *Pound/Ford: The Story of a Literary Friendship*. Ed. Brita Lindberg-Seyersted. New York: New Directions, 1982.
P/I	Ezra Pound, *Letters to Ibbertson*. Ed. V. I. Mondolfo and M. Hurley. Orono, MA: National Poetry Foundation, 1979.
P/J	Ezra Pound, *Pound/Joyce, The Letters of Ezra Pound to James Joyce*. Ed. Forrest Read. New York: New Directions, 1970.
P/L	Ezra Pound, *Pound/Lewis. The Letters of Ezra Pound and Wyndham Lewis*. Ed. Timothy Materer. New York: New Directions, 1985.
PM	Ezra Pound, *Patria Mia*. Chicago: Ralph Fletcher Seymour, 1950.
PT	Ezra Pound, *The Translations of Ezra Pound*. Intro. Hugh Kenner. London: Faber and Faber, 1984.
P/Z	Ezra Pound, *Pound/Zukofsky, Selected Letters*. Ed. Barry Ahearn. New York: New Directions, 1987.

RED   Timothy Redman, *Ezra Pound and Italian Fascism*. Cambridge: Cambridge University Press, 1991.

RP   Donald Hall, *Remembering Poets*. New York: Harper & Row, 1978. Includes "E. P. An Interview," originally in *Paris Review* 28 (1962): 22–51.

SC   Ezra Pound, *Social Credit: An Impact*. [1935.] London: Peter J. Russell, 1951.

SCh   Humphrey Carpenter, *A Serious Character, The Life of Ezra Pound*. London: Faber and Faber, 1988.

SL   Ezra Pound, *Selected Letters 1907–1941*. Ed. D. D. Paige. [1950.] New York: New Directions, 1971.

SP   Ezra Pound, *Selected Prose 1909–1965*. Ed. William Cookson. London: Faber and Faber, 1973.

SPO   Ezra Pound, *Selected Poetry*. Ed. T. S. Eliot. London: Faber & Gwyer, 1928.

SR   Ezra Pound, *The Spirit of Romance*. [1910.] New York: New Directions, 1968.

ST   Noel Stock, *Life of Ezra Pound*. 2nd edn. San Francisco: North Point Press, 1982.

Chapter 1

Life

> People quite often think me crazy when I make a jump instead of a step,
> just as if all jumps were unsound and never carried one anywhere.
>
> Pound, 1937–8

Ezra Pound loved to jump, from idea to idea, from culture to culture, from lyric
to epic. Whether on the tennis court or in the salon, he remained energized by
ideas and action. He was also outspoken and insistent: "I have never known
anyone worth a damn who wasn't irascible," Pound told Margaret Anderson
in 1917 and he fulfilled this *dicta* completely (*SL* 111). His agenda as a poet,
translator, editor, anthologist, letter-writer, essayist and *provocateur* was clear,
his plan precise: "Man reading shd. be man intensely alive. The book shd.
be a ball of light in one's hand" (*GK* 55). Vague words are an anathema, the
hard, clear statement the goal. And he does not hesitate to instruct: "Against
the metric pattern," he tells the poet Mary Barnard, "struggle toward natural
speech. You haven't *yet* got sense of quantity" (*SL* 261). The best "*mecha-
nism* for breaking up the stiffness and literary idiom *is* a different meter, the
god damn iambic magnetizes certain verbal sequences" (*SL* 260). "To break
the pentameter, that was the first heave," Pound announces in *The Cantos*
(LXXXI/538).

These statements against complacency and convention reveal the man as
much as they do his literary practice. Everything about Pound was unorthodox.
Born in the western town of Hailey, Idaho, on 30 October 1885 – his father,
Homer Pound, worked as registrar for the US Federal Land Office, recording
claims and assaying the silver and lead brought to him for its purity – Pound
became part of a family with broad American roots. A memoir by Homer
Pound celebrates *his* father, US Congressman Thaddeus Pound from Wisconsin
whose public life would enter his grandson's poetry. But US politics that saw
the Democrats replace the Republicans made Homer Pound's job in Hailey
tenuous. With his wife Isabel's happy approval – she hated life in the rugged
West – they left in 1887, first for New York and then, after securing a job at the
US Mint in Philadelphia in 1889, Pennsylvania.

After a series of homes, they settled in the suburb of Wyncote, the numerous moves adding, perhaps, to the young Pound's sense of restlessness. Throughout his life, in fact, Pound would variously live in Indiana, Venice, London, Paris, Rapallo, Washington DC (admittedly, a "guest" of the government), Brunnenburg in the Italian Alps, Rome and, finally, Venice again, where he would die in 1972.

Homer Pound's responsibilities at the Mint increased as Pound's admiration for his father's work grew, often recalling visits to the Greco-Roman-styled building in downtown Philadelphia in passages of his prose work *Indiscretions*. Gold bars and coins stacked in vaults were part of the imagery of Pound's youth and in Canto XCVII he recalls watching silver coins being shoveled into a furnace.

Pound began his formal education at Wyncote, although the absence of a public high school meant he attended the Cheltenham Military Academy, beginning in 1897. The local paper proudly recorded a 'Ray Pound' (Ray or 'Ra' was an early nickname), enrolling at the academy which required uniforms and daily drill. But the pride of his parents was unwavering, returned by the son who at one stage referred to his supportive father as "the naivest man who ever possessed sound sense," while satirizing his mother's pretensions to gentility (*Ind* 8). And like his own father who became a generous head of the family, Pound became a kind of *paterfamilias* to the modernists, offering advice, editorial instruction, support, and, when possible, money.

Before he graduated from Cheltenham, Pound made his first trip to Europe, traveling in 1898 with his Aunt Frank Weston and his mother. It foreshadowed his later fascination with European culture and his eventual move to Europe ten years later. Pound, his aunt and his mother went mostly to Italy and Spain, with a stop in Tangiers where Aunt Frank bought him a green robe which he later wore at Philadelphia social events. The first of Pound's *Pisan Cantos* (1948) recalls these early adventures. In 1902 at the age of sixteen, Pound made a second visit with Aunt Frank and his parents, stopping at London and Venice. In fact, between the ages of thirteen and twenty-six, Pound made five trips to Europe, extraordinary for a young American, but loosely duplicating the early trips made by the young Henry James. These voyages instilled in Pound a love of European culture, absorption with first-hand research and incorporation of European life in his poetry.

Pound provided an early explanation of his engagement with Europe and classical culture in 1912 when he wrote of his "struggle to find out what has been done, once for all, better than it can ever be done again, and to find out what remains for us to do . . ." (*LE* 11). In this he echoes Matthew Arnold who, in *Culture and Anarchy* (1869), defined the quest for culture as the search to locate the best that has been thought and written in the past. Both Pound and Arnold made classical literature their foundation.

Pound began the University of Pennsylvania in 1901; he was fifteen and independent. Freshmen were forbidden from wearing flashy socks but Pound disobeyed and was promptly thrown into a lily pond by second-year students, earning him the nickname "Lily Pound." But nothing would stop Pound from expressing himself, poetically or politically. His reddish golden beard also drew attention: "I make five friends for my hair, for one for myself" he once remarked (in *END* 3). At university, he compensated for his youth by being over-confident. His original goal was a Bachelor of Science degree but he gravitated to Romance languages, notably Spanish and Latin. His two closest friends were William Brooke Smith, a young artist who died in 1908 and to whom Pound would dedicate his first published work, and Hilda Doolittle, the tall, attractive blonde daughter of Penn's Professor of Astronomy, Charles Doolittle.

Pound became enamored of the woman he would rechristen for literary purposes "H. D." Both she and Pound shared a passion for classical literature and myth. His earliest volume, the vellum, hand-bound *Hilda's Book* of 1907, contains twenty-five poems for H. D. in the tradition of William Morris, Rossetti and Swinburne. They first appeared in print as the epilogue to H. D.'s *End to Torment* (1979). For a short while, the two were engaged, but H. D.'s father objected; he understood that a poet was hardly in a secure position to support his daughter and blurted out to Pound, when the poet suggested in February 1908 they might marry, "What! . . . Why, . . . you're nothing but a nomad!"[1] Also contributing to their breakup was Pound's reputation as a ladies' man. Gossip that he was involved with other women harmed him.

Pound met William Carlos Williams, a medical student, in his second year at Penn. Williams, like Pound, had literary ambitions and was exotic: his father, who was English, grew up in the West Indies, and his mother was from that region with Spanish, French and Jewish ancestry. Williams had also spent a year in Europe with his parents before beginning university. His friendship with Pound would be lifelong, Williams visiting Pound in London in 1910, Paris in the early twenties and New York in 1939 when Pound made a quick return visit. In 1958, Pound spent his last night in America at Williams' home before returning to Italy. They did not agree on everything, however, Pound objecting to Williams's defense of those poets who stayed in America, unmoved by European traditions. Williams, in turn, claimed that Pound, did little to advance US verse (*SL* 156–61). Williams would also object to Pound's racist views and anti-Semitism during the Second World War, although he defended him as a remarkable poet and worked to release him when he was arrested and jailed at St. Elizabeths Hospital in Washington, DC.

Fencing and Latin became Pound's two major interests in his second year at Penn, which resulted in mediocre grades but modest popularity. He also became disillusioned with the curriculum and proposed a transfer. He ended up at Hamilton College in Clinton, New York. This small, rural school was impressed with Pound's grasp of Latin and chess. In September 1904, he expanded his interests to Italian and Spanish, also studying Anglo-Saxon, Provençal and Hebrew, fitting in English literature when possible. Hamilton also introduced him to Dante. There, he studied *The Divine Comedy* in a bilingual edition. He also began to formulate his idea of becoming a poet, telling various professors that he planned to leave the country for Europe and begin a grand and lengthy poem, although the problem was to find a form elastic enough to include what he thought should be in a modern epic. He graduated in 1905 and returned to Penn for graduate work where, in 1906, he won a summer traveling fellowship and took off to Spain to work on *El Cid*. He also went north to southern France and visited Bordeaux, Paris and London before returning home, completing his first trip alone to Europe. On his return, he began to publish several accounts of his research and travel.

Further studies in 1906 and a renewed interest in H. D., although he was also seeing Viola Baxter and then Mary Moore, occupied Pound while concentrating on Old Provençal, Spanish drama and the *Chanson de Roland*. But he was growing impatient with academic regulations and found the university's lack of sympathy for his study of comparative literatures alienating. His fellowship was not renewed in 1907, although he was beginning to publish. "Raphaelite Latin," his first published essay, defending the pleasures of Latin, appeared in *Book News* for September 1906. The art of the language, rather than philological problems, should be the focus of study, he argued. Provincialism was the enemy, this view setting the tone for his life-long commitment to internationalism.

Pound was also continuing to write poetry, most of the manuscript of *A Lume Spento* (1908) completed before he went to Venice. In the spring of 1907, Pound heard of a position at Wabash College in Crawfordsville, Indiana, a small liberal arts school. Hired on the spot during a Philadelphia interview by the president, he left with general enthusiasm but soon found the town isolating and the bureaucracy unbearable. He taught Spanish and two French classes. Entertaining students in his rooms was discouraged so he moved to another rooming house, where he gave shelter to a penniless girl from a burlesque show he met one night in February 1908 when he went out to mail a letter. He invited her back, letting her sleep in his bed, while he slept on the floor of his study. The next morning, Pound having gone off to teach, the landladies found the girl in his bed and, within days, Pound was dismissed from the college. He returned to Wyncote, Pennsylvania, and the complicated dual romance with Mary Moore and H. D., his scandalous actions preceding him. Mary Moore rejected his proposal of marriage; H. D. accepted it but her father did not. Pound, miffed and wanting to be free of the inhibitions of American morality, responded by decamping for Europe, taking his poetry with him.

But Pound needed money and asked his father, who had a simple test. He wanted some assurance that his son had talent and sought approval of his son's work from the poet and editor Witter Bynner, who agreed to see him. A dazzlingly dressed Pound appeared at Bynner's New York offices, read his poetry out loud and impressed Bynner enough (by the clothes, perhaps, as much as the verse) for him to write a letter to Homer Pound praising the son's work. Aunt Frank also made a contribution to his travel and Pound left for Europe on St. Patrick's Day, 17 March 1908, with Mary Moore waving from the dock.

Europe was both more and less than what Pound had hoped. He arrived in Venice in April 1908 after stops at Gibraltar, Tangiers, Cadiz and Seville. He initially thought his visit would be brief, but it would be two years before he returned to America. The allure, history and culture of Venice were irresistible for the young poet who recalled his arrival and early life in Venice in Cantos III, XVII and LXXVI of his long work, *The Cantos*. He wandered about and renewed his sense of artistic purpose, forgetting the distress over the Crawfordsville incident. Venice encouraged his imagination, as two early poems, "Alma Sol Veneziae" and "San Vio," recorded. His worked lacked attention, however, so he located a printer, A. Antonini, and published his first book, the 72-page *A Lume Spento* ("With Tapers Spent"), in 150 copies. It appeared in brown paper covers in July 1908. With characteristic panache, Pound told his parents that an American reprint had to be sought, to be encouraged by several fake reviews he, himself, would write so that a recognizable publisher would want to reprint the work. The plan failed and no American edition of the book appeared until 1965.

The arrival of Kitty Heyman in Venice in June, a pianist he first met when he was at Hamilton, postponed his search for work, although he continued to write, composing in what he would label his "San Trovaso" notebook, named after his neighborhood. When *A Lume Spento* appeared, he sent fifteen copies to his father, and single copies to Williams, Mary Moore, H. D. and, most boldly, Yeats, who replied that he found the verses "charming." Pound took this as approval, telling Williams that he had "been praised by the greatest living poet" (*SL* 7–8). This support, plus the absence of work in Venice, encouraged Pound to head to London, determined to meet Yeats whom, he told his father, "had stripped English poetic of its perdamnable rhetoric . . . he has made our poetic idiom a thing pliable, a speech without inversions" (*LE* 11–12). So, in August 1908, Pound left for London, a city he found exuberant and exciting, telling William Carlos Williams in 1909 that "London, deah old Lundon, is the place for poesy" (*SL* 7).

Without losing time, Pound acquired a Reader's Ticket for the British Museum to use their vast library and made his way to the Virago Street book shop of Elkin Mathews who had the distinction of publishing Yeats's *Wind Among the Reeds* and the *Book of the Rhymer's Club*. With John Lane, Mathews had also printed *The Yellow Book*. Mathews was sympathetic to the young poet's ambitions and agreed to display Pound's first book, although not to publish the poems from the "San Trovaso" notebook. Pound spent his days writing at the British Museum but, impatient, he sought out another printer and had fifteen of his Venice poems printed as *A Quinzane for this Yule* ("Fifteen for this Yule"). One hundred copies dedicated to Kitty Heyman appeared. Mathews, to Pound's delight, ordered a second printing with several additions by Pound and with Mathew's own colophon on a re-titled front page. *Personae* was the volume's new name. Pound would use the title again for an expanded edition of 1926. The dedication, however, changed: Mary Moore of Trenton replaced Kitty Heyman. And Pound began to earn some notice from reviewers.

Just before publication, but too late to be included, Pound wrote one of his best early works, "Sestina: Altaforte," a dramatic monologue modeled on Browning, actually a rendering of a war song of the troubadour knight, Bertran de Born. The aggressive tone of the opening startled readers: "Damn it all! all this our South stinks peace" (*EPEW* 17). Pound was reinventing the sestina, removing its artificiality and decorous tone (a sestina is a poem in which the same six words, falling at the line-ends of each six-line stanza, reappear in a different order in the subsequent stanza). At the same time, Elkin Mathews aided the young poet by expanding Pound's literary circle, which grew from Ernest Rhys, editor of the Everyman series, to the novelist May Sinclair and, through her, to Ford Madox Hueffer, later to be Ford Madox Ford. Pound basked in this London light.

Ford, in fact, would play a critical role in the evolution of Pound's style. When Pound went to visit him in Giessen in 1911 to show him his latest volume, *Canzone*, Ford immediately responded by rolling on the floor. Pound's "jejune provincial effort" to learn the style of the Georgians was overwhelmingly ludicrous (*SP* 432). But that roll, Pound later wrote, "saved me at least two years, perhaps more. It sent me back to my own proper effort, namely toward using the living tongue" (*SP* 432). Pound was also now socializing widely, mostly through the circle at South Lodge where Ford was living, and having an affair with Violet

Hunt. Pound's flirtations at the time included Brigit Patmore, Phyllis Bottome and Ione de Forest. He also met D. H. Lawrence. And in 1909, through other connections, he met Mrs. Olivia Shakespear who at one time had been Yeats's mistress.

Pound began to frequent the Shakespear home, receiving, in particular, the attentions of the 22-year-old daughter, Dorothy, who quickly developed a crush on Pound who was more interested in her mother. But at this moment, he needed financial assistance not admiration; luckily, he began a lecture series in January 1909 at the Polytechnic Institute of London on the literature of southern Europe. Olivia and Dorothy Shakespear faithfully attended; others were less regular. Pound took his 5 p.m. Thursday afternoon talks seriously, often wearing a dinner jacket to provide some formality. Other times he preferred a Bohemian style with a half-opened shirt and loosely knotted tie. A black velvet jacket completed the outfit. At twenty-three, Pound at least looked the part of a poet, modeling himself on his early hero, the American expatriate painter James McNeill Whistler.

Yeats, however, still eluded him, at least until May 1909 when Olivia Shakespear took Pound to meet him at 18 Woburn Buildings in Camden. It was not until October, however, that Yeats and Pound began to spend time together (Yeats had been in Ireland throughout the summer). That October also saw Pound's new poem "The Ballad of the Goodly Fere" appear, as well as his new book, *Exultations*. But the encounter with Yeats was propitious, since the poet was casting about for several new poetic forms, although he was at first hesitant to become too involved with Pound whom he described as having a "rugged headstrong nature" and as "always hurting people's feelings." But, he added, "he has, I think, some genius and great good will."[2]

Pound encountered Yeats when the poet was questioning matters of style, seeking an unadorned method without sacrificing drama. This coincided with Pound's growing view that poetry should be "objective," eliminating excessive metaphors and adjectives. The new goal was "straight talk" (*SL* 11). When Pound returned from a short trip to America in 1910, rejecting the idea of residing there, he began to see Yeats almost daily. Monday night gatherings at Yeats's flat saw Pound play a prominent role, almost akin to host, partly recalled in Canto LXXXII. At one soirée, Pound met Bride Scratton, married but bored. He fell for her and for several years they kept up a liaison, although there were other women as well.

During a short trip to Paris to visit his pianist friend Walter Morse Rummel, Pound met Margaret Cravens, an American who had studied piano with Ravel. She admired Pound's writing and free spirit and began to provide a subsidy so that he could complete *The Spirit of Romance*, a book drawn from his London lectures. With this new source of income, he was also now able to cancel his regular payments from his father. He even felt confident enough to ask Dorothy Shakespear's father for permission to marry his daughter. He refused, citing among other things Pound's unstable finances. His association with Cravens strengthened and at one point she commissioned portraits of both of them. But on 1 June 1912, she committed suicide shortly after learning that Walter Morse Rummel, possibly her lover, was engaged to someone else. Pound's Imagist poem, "His Vision of a Certain Lady Post Mortem" (1914), records a dream about Cravens.

In 1910, Pound also went to Italy and, for the first time, visited Sirmione on Lago di Garda. This area, where Catullus had a villa, became one of his favorite spots, the land thrusting out into the large, unnaturally blue lake surrounded by the Italian Alps. It would be a site of significance, where Dorothy's own artistic inspiration rekindled, where Pound met Joyce and where he would re-launch *The Cantos* in June 1922. During his 1910 visit, he corrected proof for *The Spirit of Romance* and wrote several poems. Olivia and Dorothy Shakespear soon joined him there and, in May, all three went on to Venice. By June, however, he was on the *Lusitania* traveling from Liverpool to New York.

His visit was a time of reassessment. Should he stay in America or return to Europe? He quickly found there was less work for a poet in America than in England or Italy, and almost no inspiration. He re-met H. D. who followed him from Philadelphia to New York but he showed little interest in her. He also saw Kitty Heyman and contacted both Mary Moore and Viola Baxter. Through Yeats's father, John B. Yeats, a painter then in New York, Pound met the lawyer and patron, John Quinn. A friendship developed and Quinn would later visit Pound when he went to Paris in 1923. A memorable photograph taken in Pound's studio at that time records Joyce, Pound, Ford Madox Ford and Quinn standing together. While Pound was in the States, Walter Morse Rummel visited and Pound expanded his interest in music, which he turned into something profitable when he returned to England in February 1911: he became a music critic publishing under the pseudonym of William Atheling. Music would also play a greater part in his understanding of poetry, which in 1918 he defined as "a composition of words set to music" (*LE* 437). Arnold Dolmetsch, George Antheil and, of course, Olga Rudge, the American violinist who would have a long relationship with Pound, were all deeply immersed in music as composers or performers.

Pound spent some time in New York exploring the possibility of a literary career but he did not take to the city, nor to its writers. He felt commerce controlled its culture, while the architecture seemed inauthentic. He expanded these views in a series of articles he titled *Patria Mia* published in the *New Age* in

1912–13. He had returned to London, but stayed briefly, taking off for Paris and the world of music. He spent time with Cravens and Rummel's brother, a cellist, as well as days at the Bibliothèque National with its collection of Troubadour manuscripts. He focused most of his energy on completing a translation of the sonnets and ballads of Cavalcanti, the fourteenth-century Italian poet of the *dolce stil novo* ("sweet new school") of poetry, and completing the manuscript of his own work he would publish as *Canzoni* (1911), dedicated to Olivia and Dorothy Shakespear. Before returning to England, he visited Milan, Freiberg and Giessen where he visited Ford.

In London, he shared his enthusiasm for Cavalcanti with T. E. Hulme who thought Pound needed to widen his views and introduced him to A. R. Orage, editor of the *New Age*, a socialist paper devoted to furthering the arts. Liberal, if not radical, in its views, the paper published Shaw, Hulme, H. G. Wells, Katherine Mansfield and others, providing a new outlet for Pound. Essays, poems, music criticism, art criticism and translations by Pound soon began to appear in the *New Age*, one of the most important works his rendering of the Anglo-Saxon poem "The Seafarer." His vigorous translation brought criticism and praise, his liberal view of translation expressed in the statement "dont bother about the WORDS, translate the MEANING."[3] By 1912, Pound seemed to be everywhere, as poet, editor, essayist and polemicist.

One of Pound's most revolutionary acts occurred in the tea room of the British Museum. In the early fall of 1912, Pound read H. D.'s poem "Hermes of the Ways." After slashing through the text, he rapidly wrote at the bottom "H. D. Imagiste" and a movement was born. At the time, he was Foreign Correspondent of Harriet Monroe's *Poetry* magazine in Chicago, to which he sent the poem. Of course, Imagism did not suddenly emerge full-bloom in a London tea room, even one in such august surroundings as the British Museum. It was the result of Pound's study of the Provençal poets and Dante, with their emphasis on the precise, the detailed. T. E. Hulme's writing and the French Symbolists also contributed to his position, partly expressed as "go in fear of abstractions. Do not retell in mediocre verse what has already been done in good prose" (*LE* 3–5). Pound's 1914 anthology, *Des Imagistes*, demonstrated the Imagist work of poets as diverse as H. D., Williams, Ford, Joyce and Amy Lowell, with whom he would soon battle over the concept.

Pound's profile grew when he became poetry editor of Dora Marsden and Harriet Shaw Weaver's the *New Freewoman*, soon to be renamed *The Egoist*. This liberal journal would become an active source of new ideas and writing. In 1913, he also discovered Robert Frost, reviewing Frost's first book for *Poetry*, taking credit for boosting his reputation (*SL* 62). Pound, however, thought nothing of improving the American's poems, but when he told Frost he had shortened a poem of fifty words to forty-eight, Frost angrily replied that he had spoiled his meter, idiom and idea (*SCh* 201). Pound at this time also befriended the French sculptor Henri Gaudier-Brzeska and Mrs. Ernest Fenollosa, widow of the distinguished Orientalist. The former would introduce Pound to a new aesthetic of direct, geometric art expressed through his own solid but expressive bust of Pound, undertaken in 1914. Pound admired Gaudier-Brzeska's chiseled work, finding in it a metaphor for his own writing, especially in "Homage to Sextus Propertius," *Mauberley* and *The Cantos*. The accumulated lines and allusions in Pound almost stand on one another, as do the hard-cut lines in Gaudier-Brzeska's work. Pound's new form is an "arrangement of masses in relation, . . . energy cut into stone," similar to Gaudier-Brzeska's style (*GB* 110). The sculptor's death in battle in June 1915 was a shock to Pound who would publish a memoir of his friend and his art the following year.

The notebooks and manuscripts given to Pound by the widow of the Orientalist Ernest Fenollosa introduced him to the world of the Chinese ideogram. Pound was fascinated and shared his interest with Yeats, while adapting a series of first-level translations by Fenollosa into the attenuated poetry of *Cathay* (1915). Pound's editing and publishing Fenollosa "The Chinese Written Character as a Medium for Poetry" several years later was instrumental in advancing Pound's own aesthetic and poetic practice.

The year 1913, when Pound received the Fenollosa materials, was significant in another way: it was the first of three winters Pound would spend with Yeats, acting as his principal secretary, at Stone Cottage in Sussex. The two writers exchanged ideas about art, Pound in particular introducing Yeats to Noh drama and Chinese poetry, the result of his study of the Fenollosa papers. Pound was actually revising Fenollosa's draft translations of Japanese Noh dramas at that time. Yeats read these versions and found inspiration for his own theatre pieces. Pound, in turn, became interested in Yeats's occult studies and began to read widely in esoteric literature. He also read Browning's *Sordello* out loud to Yeats and initiated steady work on what would become his long poem, *The Cantos*. Additionally, Yeats introduced Pound to the work of Joyce, while Pound introduced Yeats to the work of Eliot. Yeats would later acknowledge Pound's help: "to talk over a poem with him is like getting you to put a sentence into dialect. All becomes clear and natural" he told Lady Gregory.[4]

In 1913, Pound wrote to the young James Joyce, at Yeats's suggestion, for a poem to include in his new anthology, *Des Imagistes* (1914). Joyce sent "I Hear an Army" and an epistolary friendship began until the two met at Sirmione, Italy, in June 1920. Pound began to play an important part in Joyce's personal as well as literary life, organizing the move of the Joyces to Paris and introducing Joyce to Sylvia Beach who would publish *Ulysses* in February 1922.

He also became instrumental in getting *A Portrait of the Artist* published in *The Egoist.*

While whirling through literary London, Pound was also solidifying his relationship with Dorothy Shakespear (and her father, unhappy about the union): they married on 20 April 1914 and spent their honeymoon at Stone Cottage. But Pound was far from settled, at least artistically, developing Vorticism with Wyndham Lewis, expressed through their magazine BLAST, first published in June 1914. In September, his essay "Vorticism" appeared, the term expressing the "energized past" represented by a work of art. "Futurism," a competing aesthetic originating with Marinetti, was diffuse: it "is the disgorging spray of a vortex with no drive behind it. DISPERSAL" (*EPVA* 151). Vorticism is focused, primary energy represented in painting by Kandinsky, in poetry by H. D. (*EPVA* 152). In an essay on Vortographs, geometric photographs by Alvin Langdon Coburn, Pound writes that "the vorticist principle is that a painting is an expression by means of an arrangement of form and colour in the same way that a piece of music is an expression . . . of an arrangement of sound." Sculpture makes use, for example, of "masses defined by planes" (*EPVA* 154–5).

In his essay "Vorticism," Pound also clarifies differences between Imagism and Vorticism. The former "does not use images *as ornaments.* The image is itself the speech" he writes (*EPEW* 285). Imagism is, furthermore, oriented around "the luminous detail," the telling particular that he mentions in the first part of his prose series, "I Gather the Limbs of Osiris," published in December 1911 (*SP* 21). Later in the essay, he identifies the "interpreting detail[s]" as facts that reveal the intelligence of an age. Such facts govern knowledge "as the switchboard governs an electric circuit"; the artist's job is to seek out "the luminous detail" and present it without comment (*SP* 23). All detail is not of equal value, he reminds us, nor are literary texts. In a leap of logic, he equates "luminous detail" with particular texts and authors who may illuminate a time. Hence, his stress on *individual* texts in his criticism (*SP* 24). This insight relates to Pound's historical method which lies not in the accumulation of masses of data, but in the examination of only those pieces that represent significant changes in outlook or the configuration of an era. Vorticism, in turn, is "an intensive art" and this intensity of primary forms causes other "form to come into being" (*EPEW* 287, 289). The image, he repeats, "is not an idea. It is a radiant node or cluster; it is what I can, and must perforce, call a VORTEX, from which and through which, and into which ideas are constantly rushing" (*EPEW* 289).

In September 1914, the same month Pound published his Vorticism essay, he met the young American poet T. S. Eliot and immediately sensed his talent.

He quickly told Harriet Monroe that Eliot was the only American adequately prepared to write: "he has actually trained himself *and* modernized himself *on his own*" he enthused (*SL* 40). He admired "The Love Song of J. Alfred Prufrock" which Eliot had sent to him and posted it immediately to *Poetry*, calling it "the best poem I have yet had or seen from an American" (*SL* 40). That month he also negotiated for the publication of *A Portrait of the Artist* by Joyce in *The Egoist*.

In London Pound continued to act as literary manager and cultural impresario overseeing publications and editorial developments. Ideas for new magazines, journals, programs and even anthologies burst forth and he saw his role clearly – no less than "to keep alive a certain group of advancing poets, to set the arts in their rightful place as the acknowledged guide and lamp of civilization" (1915; *SL* 48). When *The Egoist* Press published Eliot's first book, *Prufrock and Other Observations*, for example, Pound paid the printing costs. He took his job seriously. During one week in March 1916, for example, in addition to book reviewing, he acted as executor to the Gaudier-Brzeska estate, oversaw the packing of a Vorticist exhibition for display in New York, made a selection of the letters of Yeats's father for publication and helped to produce a play by W. B. Yeats (*SL* 72). Additionally, he was trying to revive *The Egoist* and was expecting proofs any day of *Certain Noble Plays of Japan*, published by the Cuala Press. In the letter in which he reports all of this, he also tells the recipient that she should prepare an article on this new theatre, or, as he calls it, "theatreless drama about which there'll be a good deal to say soon" because – and here is the news – "Yeats is making a new start on the foundation of these Noh dramas" (*SL* 72).

But within a year, England provided less stimulation. While he was continuing to publish – *Catholic Anthology* (1915), *Certain Noble Plays of Japan* (1916) – and placing such texts as portions of Joyce's *Ulysses* with the *Little Review*, and his own "Three Cantos" with *Poetry* (1917), Pound was finding London culturally stale. Major C. H. Douglas introduced him to Social Credit which he found of interest, and his music, art and literary criticism continued to appear in *the New Age*. But southern France and Italy offered more inspiration. London was no more than people carrying "particles of knowledge and gossip, wearing you away little by little," a process he described more negatively in his poem "Portrait d'une Femme."[5] In June 1919 he tells John Quinn that, after two weeks, he was fired as drama critic from the *Outlook* and his work had been turned down "by about every editor in England and America . . . circumstances too dull to narrate." England, in short, no longer had any "intellectual *life*" (*SL* 151, 158). In *Guide to Kulchur*, he would further castigate the country and approvingly quote Hemingway in one of his Rome radio broadcasts, who declared in 1922 that Pound was "the ONLY American who ever got out of England alive" (*GK* 228; *EPS* 245).

Hugh Selwyn Mauberley, appearing in June 1920, underlines Pound's disillusionment with England, the year also marking his departure, carrying in his pocket a letter from Thomas Hardy concerning the title of "Propertius" (see Canto LXXX/520). By January 1921, he and Dorothy moved to France, eventually taking up residence in Paris. In France, Pound found a new circle: Cocteau, Picabia, Picasso, Stein, Brancusi, Hemingway, plus Nancy Cunard and Natalie Barney whose salon was notorious for its mix of culture and sex. His friendship with Joyce, living in Paris for nearly a year, continued, while he now concentrated on an opera, *Le Testament de Villon*, which would actually be performed in Paris in June 1926. In November 1921, Eliot, on his way to Switzerland as part of his recovery from a nervous breakdown (necessitating a three-month leave from Lloyd's Bank where he was then working), showed the typescript of *The Waste Land* to Pound. In response to some likely harsh remarks, Eliot redrafted parts and added the section "What the Thunder Said" when in Lausanne.

On his return through Paris, Eliot showed the now nineteen-page poem to Pound, who approved the changes. Eliot left Pound a typescript and, by January 1922, Pound finished his careful re-reading and editing and returned the fully marked up and revised text – with cuts, transpositions and improvements – to Eliot in London, writing "Complimenti, you bitch. I am wracked by the seven jealousies" (*SL* 169; *SCh* 405–7 summarizes the changes). In Paris, Pound boxed with Hemingway, met William Bird who would start the Three Mountains Press (and publish several of Pound's works) and promoted Hemingway's early prose vignettes, *in our time*, edited by Pound, which Bird would publish in 1924. The London and Paris years, roughly 1909–23, from *Personae* to the "Malatesta Cantos" (*Criterion*, July 1923), were Pound's most productive.

On a return from a walking tour with Hemingway in Italy in 1923, Pound met the American violinist Olga Rudge in Paris at Natalie Barney's. He had heard her play in London at the end of 1920 but did not meet her. Attracted to her energy, good looks and confidence, plus their common passion for music, Pound began a difficult 49-year relationship, despite being married to Dorothy. At this time, he was also developing more extended sections of *The Cantos*, drawing on research from a 1922 trip to Italy to compose one of the first discrete sections of the work, the Malatesta Cantos (VIII–XI), so called after Sigismundo Malatesta, fifteenth-century ruler of Rimini.

But even Paris began to pale and Pound and Dorothy began to think of moving to Italy, making a trip there in February 1924 and settling permanently at the small seaside town of Rapallo east and slightly south of Genoa in October 1924.

In a 1931 interview, he explained his choice as an absorption with the impact of Italy in civilizing Europe – twice (the Renaissance and through Fascism). Reflecting on his admiration of Mussolini and Fascism, he tells a reporter that "without a strong Italy, I don't see the possibility of a balanced Europe" (in *RED* 76). The new Italy had the potential to unite power and intelligence as it did in the fifteenth century.

Back in England, Pound's reputation faded as Richard Aldington made clear in a letter to Amy Lowell in 1925: "I don't know if he has retained any reputation in America, but here he is almost forgotten, and as the rest of us go up, he goes down."[6] Pound's strident Fascism of the 1930s marginalized him further, understood now by a generation of younger poets as the views of an extremist and crank.

Italian life was isolating but not unpleasant for Pound, who wrote, played tennis and got settled in his top-floor apartment overlooking the harbor of Rapallo, whose only previous English writer of note was Max Beerbohm. "Il poeta," Pound's Italian nickname, was soon joined by Yeats who spent nearly a year there, partly because of illness. Soon, Olga Rudge was in Italy and in July 1925 gave birth to her daughter with Pound, Mary, in the Italian Tyrol. Dorothy, understandably upset, would give birth to a son, Omar, the following year in Paris following a voyage to Egypt (Hemingway accompanied her to the hospital). The father was not Pound, although he legally adopted the child.

Pound now began to edit his short-lived journal *Exile* (four issues, 1927–8) and spend more time in Venice where Olga owned a small house at 252 Dorsoduro, just off the calle Querini. By 1928, Pound was flourishing, with *A Draft of the Cantos 17–27* published in London in a deluxe edition and his *Selected Poems* edited by Eliot published by Faber. His mother and father also visited him in Rapallo and enjoyed it so much they decided to move there. The following year, Olga gave up her apartment in Paris and moved permanently to Venice; she would later move to a small home above Rapallo in Sant'Ambrogio, up the *salita* or path which Pound would frequently walk. Pound remained creatively active, continuing with his long poem and writing new prose works including *How to Read* (1931), *Profile: An Anthology* (1932) and an *ABC of Economics* (1933). Underscoring his increasing political and economic commentary were columns he wrote for *Il Mare*, a Rapallo paper, and his growing admiration for Mussolini whom he would meet in Rome in January 1933, an event he recounts in Canto LXI.

In Rapallo, visitors, sometimes disciples, now began to appear in what was loosely labeled the "Ezuversity": the young British poet Basil Bunting, the American poet Louis Zukofsky, and the exceptionally tall Harvard student who, on Pound's advice, would return to America and begin a publishing company, James Laughlin. His New Directions, founded in 1936, became one of the leading avant-garde publishers in America and has continued to keep Pound's work in print. Pound's energy was prodigious, as he himself noted in a letter at this time to Harriet Monroe, in which he outlines what he has been trying to teach her for the past twenty years or so as she contemplates the end of *Poetry* magazine because of financial problems. He urges her to continue, wonders if the magazine's guarantors truly hate him, and ends with "Now, lie right down and git a bit of rest. I am not going to essplode any dynamite till I get an answer" (*SL* 237).

Olga Rudge pursued her career in music, Pound accompanying her whenever possible, whether it was to the Salzburg musical festival or the summer music school at Siena founded by Count Chigi. Soon, she would be promoting and playing the work of Vivaldi, Pound taking a keen interest in his compositions. In the mid-1930s, while Mussolini's Fascist party ruled Italy and invaded Abyssinia, Pound became more vocal in his political opinions, publishing *Social Credit* and *Jefferson and/or Mussolini*, both in 1935; *Polite Essays* appeared in 1937. His support of Fascism was unquestioned as he made clear in a series of short-wave radio broadcasts he offered to America, beginning in 1941 and continuing on a more-or-less regular basis until 1943.

Cantos continued to appear, as well as his work on Confucius. By 1938 his *Guide to Kulchur* was published, a summary of what should be known and what should be discarded by intelligent and aware individuals. When signs of war increased, he traveled to America in April 1939 in an attempt to warn the country, lobbying a series of US Congressmen. He mixed one or two literary events with his politicking, giving a reading at Harvard in May. In June he received an honorary degree from Hamilton College. He returned to Italy at the end of that month and, shortly after, published the pamphlet *What Is Money For?* Soon, he met the philosopher George Santayana in Venice and appeared in such diverse publications as the *Japan Times* (Tokyo), and, more consistently, *Il Meridiano di Roma*.

At this time, work on *The Cantos* halted, although in 1940 the so-called "Chinese Cantos" appeared in *Cantos LII–LXXI*. His regular Rome radio broadcasts become more highly critical of Roosevelt, the war effort and Jews. As the war spread, he took refuge in Rapallo, but still made dangerous trips to broadcast in Rome. In 1942, his father died and his daughter Mary, now seventeen, continued with an Italian translation of separate Cantos. Broadcasting again in 1943, Pound was now indicted by a Grand Jury in Washington, DC, for treason. The day before the indictment, on 25 July 1943, Mussolini was deposed. In September, after an unsuccessful visit to Rome, Pound began a dangerous,

450-mile trek, partly by rail, partly on foot, to the Tyrol to see his daughter. Italy was now occupied by the Germans. During his visit, Pound confessed to his daughter that he had a son, living in England.

By 1944, the Germans ordered Pound and Dorothy to leave Rapallo; they moved up the mountain to Sant'Ambrogio, the hilltop town above the city, to live (awkwardly) with Olga. At this time, Pound wrote the two "Italian Cantos" (LXXII and LXXIII) published in *La Marina Repubblicana* in early 1945, but not in the complete *Cantos* until 1985. Mussolini, fleeing his new republic of Salò in the north, was captured and killed in April 1945. The next month, Germany surrendered Italy to the Allies. Pound, now sixty, walked down the hill to American troops to turn himself in. They didn't know what to do with him; he returned home, but was then arrested by two Italian partisans and eventually handed over to American troops in Genoa where he was formally detained and sent to Pisa and the US Army Disciplinary Training Center, essentially a prisoner camp.

Before his capture, Pound managed to slip into his pocket a copy of the Confucian classics he had been translating and a Chinese–English dictionary, as well as a small seed from the *salita*. For nearly two and half weeks at Pisa, Pound lived in a solitary steel pen exposed to the elements before he experienced a physical breakdown. He was moved to the medical compound where he slowly recovered. To maintain his well-being and mental health, he worked on his translation of Confucius and began to compose what would be called *The Pisan Cantos* (LXXIV–LXXXIV), one of the most accessible sections of the entire poem.

On 16 November 1945, Pound was secretly taken from Pisa's DTC to Rome where he began a flight to Washington, DC, to stand trial for treason. He was arraigned on the 27th but a trial was postponed, pending a psychiatric examination. By mid-December, he was found mentally unfit to stand trial and committed to St. Elizabeths Hospital for the Criminally Insane. He would remain there for the next twelve-and-a-half years. In 1946, T. S. Eliot visited him, and a long list of distinguished writers, politicians and journalists followed, including Marianne Moore, Allan Tate, Randall Jarrell, Thornton Wilder, Stephen Spender, Robert Lowell, Katherine Anne Porter, Louis Zukofsky, Langston Hughes and Charles Olson, as well as Edith Hamilton, Marshall McLuhan and Hugh Kenner. Elizabeth Bishop published a poem "Visit to St. Elizabeths"; Charles Olson published his own account of seeing Pound in 1975. During this time, Pound continued to work, completing a revision of *The Pisan Cantos* which appeared in July 1948 – igniting a new controversy.

That year the Library of Congress prepared to award its first Bollingen Prize for Poetry and, after heated debate, chose *The Pisan Cantos* which was competing against Book Two of William Carlos Williams's *Paterson*. The committee, which included Conrad Aiken, W. H. Auden, T. S. Eliot, Robert Lowell, Katherine Anne Porter, Karl Shapiro, Allen Tate and Robert Penn Warren, needed two ballots for its decision. Anticipating strong public reaction, they prepared a press release in which they stated that to consider elements other than poetic achievement would diminish the importance of the award. The public did not agree: to give an award to an anti-Semite and Fascist sympathizer accused of treason seemed a betrayal of American ideals.

A national outcry followed, the headline in the *New York Times* reminding readers "Pound, in Mental Clinic, Wins Prize for Poetry Penned in Treason Cell" (20 February 1949). The headline was, of course, misleading since Pound had written most of the poems before he arrived in Washington. Congressmen, literary critics and poets battled over the correctness of the award, with magazines, radio programs and newspapers offering numerous contradictory opinions. Editorials, forums, and commentaries from several of the jurors (appearing in the *Partisan Review*) dominated the discussion. A pamphlet appeared challenging the conservative views opposing Pound's receipt of the award. Some declared Pound not mad at all while others, like Congressman Jacob Javits, called for a congressional inquiry into the circumstances surrounding the award. Told of the award just before the public announcement, Pound prepared a statement for the press but chose not to release it. It read "No comment from the Bug House" (in *SCh* 793).

Probably no book of twentieth-century American poetry created more controversy than *The Pisan Cantos*. In the end, the $1,000 award, subsidized by the Mellon family of Pittsburgh, went to Pound but the administration of the award shifted from the Library of Congress to Yale. Ironically, the year Pound's controversial book was published, his close friend T. S. Eliot won an uncontested award: the Nobel Prize for Literature. In the meantime, Dorothy Pound had, herself, taken up residence in Washington and visited Pound daily – except when Olga and then Mary came to see him. Pound also found a new disciple, Sheri Martinelli, a painter who became something of a third partner for him.

Portions of *The Cantos* continued to appear, notably *Section: Rock Drill* in 1955, as well as new work: *The Classic Anthology Defined by Confucius*, plus Pound's translation of Sophocles' *Women of Trachis* (1956). By 1958, a petition to release the 72-year-old Pound was finally granted by a US District Court, a drive spearheaded by Robert Frost, Archibald MacLeish, Hemingway and Eliot. Legally in charge of him on his release was Dorothy. Officially discharged on 7 May 1958, Pound revisited his childhood home in Wyncote, and spent his last night in America with William Carlos Williams. By 9 July he was in Naples, having returned with Dorothy and Marcella Spann (a new follower of Pound's), declaring to reporters that "all America is an insane asylum" and giving the Fascist salute for cameramen.

Pound, Dorothy and Marcella headed for Brunnenburg, the castle his daughter Mary and her husband purchased in 1948 in northern Italy, and a period of tension began that, after a few months, saw Marcella depart, although not before all three took an apartment in Rapallo. By January 1960 an ailing Pound went by himself to Rome, returning to Dorothy in Rapallo by May as a period of silence and depression descended. He entered and left various clinics until his health improved but by then he had chosen to move in with Olga at Sant'Ambrogio, alternating between there and calle Querini in Venice. At this point, several of his closest and most important friends began to die, William Carlos Williams in March 1963 and T. S. Eliot in January 1965. Despite his age, he decided to attend the memorial service for Eliot at Westminster Abbey and then, spontaneously, to visit Yeats's widow in Dublin. That summer, he attended the Spoleto Festival and publicly read poems by Marianne Moore and Robert Lowell. He turned eighty that October but visited Paris, attending a performance of Beckett's *Endgame*.

In 1967, Pound visited Joyce's grave in Zurich and that summer Allen Ginsberg came to see him in Venice. His *Selected Cantos* appeared. Two years later, Pound unexpectedly arrived in New York with Olga to attend a meeting of the Academy of American Poets and the opening exhibition of the typescript he corrected of *The Waste Land*. Laughlin, surprised by his guests, rescued Pound and Olga from an inappropriate Manhattan hotel and took them to his Greenwich Village apartment and then on to Hamilton College where Laughlin was to receive an honorary degree. Pound sat on the stage and received a standing ovation. That year, 1969, *Drafts & Fragments of Cantos CX–CXVII* appeared, partly to counter a pirated edition that was published in 1967. Pound returned to Venice, where he died on 1 November 1972, one day past his eighty-seventh birthday. His grave is on the isle of San Michele, not far from Stravinsky and Diaghilev. Dorothy Pound would die in 1973 in England and Olga Rudge in March 1996. She is buried next to Pound.

Chapter 2

Context

> Have you met Ezra Pound? . . . The Americans, young literary men,
> whom I know found him surly, supercilious and grumpy. I liked him
> myself very much.   John B. Yeats to his son, W. B. Yeats, 1910

When Ezra Pound arrived in London he was greeted as an American cowboy, a brash outsider offering poetry *Punch* satirized as blending "the imagery of the unfettered West, the vocabulary of Wardour Street, and the sinister abandon of Borgiac Italy" (in *EPM* 174). Outspoken, oddly dressed – he would occasionally wear a sombrero for a 1909 lecture series – Pound was, nonetheless, self-assured. His appearance was operatic and poetic at the same time, preferring flowing capes and open-necked shirts, but his speech was "Amerukun," filled with idioms and neologisms unheard of in London. As one observer wrote, with "his rimless *pince nez*, his Philadelphian accent and his startling costume, part of which was a single turquoise earring, [he] contrived to look 'every inch a poet.'"[1] But his unorthodox ideas and direct approach to art made him more than an image as he challenged the stodginess of late Victorian culture and the indulgencies of the Decadents as he set out a modernist map that T. S. Eliot, Yeats, Joyce, Lewis and others would follow.

An afternoon visit to the poet Wilfrid Scawen Blunt in Sussex on 18 January 1914 illustrates how Pound first straddled and then rattled the age, causing Yeats to remark that "Pound has a desire personally to insult the world."[2] The purpose of the afternoon was to acknowledge Blunt and his contributions to poetry. On the day of the visit, in the company of Yeats, Richard Aldington, T. Sturge Moore. F. S. Flint, and Victor Plarr, Pound and the others honored the poet with a small reliquary box designed by Gaudier-Brzeska containing poems by the poets. Blunt was gracious in accepting the gift but turned the image of a naked Egyptian woman on the box to the wall the next day and commented that in the poems themselves he could not recognize "anything but word puzzles" (in McDiarmid 164). Pound was the anonymous author of all of them, although Blunt did not know it (GAL C131).

Called "the peacock dinner" after the chief item on the menu, the gathering symbolizes the crossing of the old poetic world with the new. A photograph taken at the event provides a visual genealogy of modernism which Pound remembered in Canto LXXXI of *The Pisan Cantos*. Flanking a very bearded Blunt (standing in the center of the photo and wearing a lightly colored wool suit), is Yeats, off to the right, in a dark, double-breasted suit, left hand raised to his lapel. To Blunt's left stands a relaxed Pound, hands in pocket with wide-collared shirt overflowing his jacket collar, nonchalantly displaying a loosely tied tie. Next to Pound in the semi-circle is Richard Aldington and then F. S. Flint. On the opposite side next to Yeats is T. Sturge Moore and, at the end, Victor Plarr, all in well-cut suits. Pound, exaggerating his casual flair, is the only one wearing spats.

In "Homage to Wilfrid Blunt," appearing in *Poetry* in March 1914, Pound recounts the meeting and reprints the poems in homage signed by "the committee" and read at the event by Pound. Pound also sent a copy of the photograph to Alice Corbin Henderson, associate editor of *Poetry* in Chicago. *The Times* of London for 20 January 1914 reported the event, framed by a brief account of air flights above the Nile and "Boxing in France" (see McDiarmid 169). The confluence of Blunt with the younger figures representing the Imagists, the soon-to-be Vorticists and Yeats, all engineered by Pound, symbolizes the changing of the literary guard which the next several years would confirm. But preparation for this shift started long before 1914.

In 1908, the year Pound published his first book, *A Lume Spento*, Gertrude Stein also published *Three Lives* and Arnold Bennett *The Old Wives' Tale*. The contrast is instructive because it suggests the exchange occurring between Edwardian realism and early modernist experimentation. Stein was attempting something new, asymmetric and original. Bennett was continuing with the old: a stable narrative and clear sense of closure. The next year, when Pound published *Personae* (1909), all hell seemed to break loose as experimentation and irregularity infiltrated painting and music: Matisse completed *The Dance*, Mahler, *Symphony No.9*, and Schönberg, *Five Orchestral Pieces*, expanded the following year with the Post-Impressionist exhibition in London and the premier of Stravinsky's *The Firebird* ballet. Virginia Woolf may have been right when she wrote that "in or about December 1910, human character changed." Or, as she wrote in her diary after a Bloomsbury party some years later, recording a kind of modernist behavior: "we collided, when we met: went pop, used Christian names, flattered, praised & thought (or I did) of Shakespeare . . . We were all easy & gifted & friendly."[3] Formality was gone; informality and fresh ideas were in.

A new aesthetic also emerged, one partly defined by the rediscovery of the mythopoetic and the primitive. T. S. Eliot's essay "Ulysses, Order and Myth" outlines the former, Picasso's work the latter. Appearing in the November 1923 edition of the *Dial*, Eliot's essay pursues the Odyssean links between Joyce's novel and Homer. But, more importantly, Eliot articulated what Pound was doing in *The Cantos*, grafting earlier periods of history, specifically the classical, onto the modern era. Or, in Eliot's words related to Joyce, fashioning "a continuous parallel between contemporaneity and antiquity" which had the importance "of a scientific discovery." He stressed that the Homeric parallels, what would be called the mythic method, were a way of "ordering, of giving shape and significance to the immense panorama of futility and anarchy which is contemporary history" – virtually a description of the technique of the *Cantos*.[4] In attaching the Provençal past to the classical, as well as Renaissance, world, Pound performed an identical task.

This unexpected linking of cultures to one another, a hallmark of modernism, was evident in Picasso's use of primitivism, which *Les Demoiselles d'Avignon* of 1907 illustrates through its angular bodies with African connotations. Picasso seemed to dismantle conventional erotic figures, with bodies lacking a formal aesthetic unity through the absence of a conventional perspective. Stravinsky's *Rite of Spring* (1913), a work creating immense reaction, furthered the seemingly unstructured presentations of Stein, Joyce, Pound and Lewis. The dissonant and unharmonic music created a physical response of outrage, the audience not knowing how to respond to sounds in which "from the first to last bar of the work there is not a note that one expects."[5] But this may be the point, expressed later in the work of the Orientalist Pound would study, Ernest Fenollosa. In his important essay "The Chinese Written Character as a Medium for Poetry," edited by Pound, Fenollosa writes, "relations are more real and more important than the things which they relate" (*EPEW* 320). To make something new is to fashion the unexpected and in the process express *unresolved* conflicts: Regularity and unity have been rejected by irregularity and fragmentation.

London before and during the First World War was a city without much of an avant-garde tradition. It resisted the outrageous; tolerating the bohemian was about as far as it would go. In the aftermath of the Oscar Wilde trial of May 1895, nineties' aestheticism was pushed out, while unthreatening, conventional poetry and the social novel were reinstated. James, Galsworthy, Bennett and H. G. Wells ruled. Until the arrival of "Les Jeunes," as Ford Madox Ford called them – Lewis, Pound, Joyce, Eliot, H. D. – as well as Virginia Woolf, D. H. Lawrence and Dorothy Richardson, art remained uninspired, conservative.

Bohemia, however, quickly became a catalyst for this movement eventually called modernism. In cafes, studios, bookshops, tea rooms and editorial offices, the new expressed itself in the unorthodox treatment of text, image and structure, as well as being anti-mimetic, emphasizing in particular simultaneity. Subjectivity re-appeared not only in literary and artistic practice but in dress. Costume, a weapon against bourgeois convention, equaled the claims of artistic originality, extending in part Théophile Gautier's appearance in a scarlet satin waistcoat with thick long hair cascading down his back. A hero of Pound's, the French poet and journalist linked bohemianism with dandyism. One had to look like an artist to be one, in London even more so, to separate oneself from the masses. Non-conformity reigned. Three of Pound's heroes who emulated this were visually distinctive: Rossetti, Swinburne and Whistler.

Identities were shifting and a new cosmopolitanism aligned itself with the modernist movement which Wyndham Lewis emulated. Lewis had spent time in Paris, Spain, Germany and Holland between 1902 and 1908, striking Pound as a rare bird, "an English man who has achieved the triumph of being also a European" (*LE* 424). Pound also achieved this, as various photographs of him throughout his career would confirm, one striking image that of 1928 taken by Bill Brandt in Vienna and representing Pound as a European gangster with a dark fedora pulled down over his eyes and his topcoat collar turned up. This defiant, *noir* Pound is all determination as he provokes his viewer, daring him to question his beliefs. The image is more of a literary hitman than poet, the beard now overshadowed by his hat, casting a ring of darkness, although the upturned collar of the coat does not quite hide the flamboyant white collar of his shirt. The tight focus on Pound's face and the chiaroscuro effect adds an eloquent foreboding to the picture. The photograph evokes Pound's late remark that he was "the last American living the tragedy of Europe" (*RP* 244). This was a time when reinvention seemed the norm for Americans: T. S. Eliot submerged his American identity in a cosmopolitan Englishness that saw him constantly with bowler and furled umbrella. H. D. became an "Imagist" dressing as if in a classical world. Whistler with his capes and walking sticks was their prototype, balanced by the dark-suited, unrelaxed presence of Henry James.

These habits reflect the period's interest in the mask, a term often applied in relation to Wilde and Yeats, but taking on a new shape with Pound through a persona. This reaction to the self-indulgent subjectivity of earlier periods allowed one to adopt a series of personalities and contributed to the supposed objectivism of modernism. Wearing a mask also had the effect of depersonalizing the poet. At the same time as a persona hides the actual person, it may also, paradoxically, reveal elements of the unmasked self. Dramatizing the voice of another becomes an important feature of Pound's poetry especially through *Hugh Selwyn Mauberley* (1920).

Another measure of the new energy of modernism was the rise of the little magazine which provided a public, as well as international, face for the movement, although a modest one. No longer were institutionalized nineteenth-century periodicals like the *Edinburgh Review* or the *Westminster Review* or *Fraser's* determining cultural values or taste. Starting with *The Yellow Book* and moving on to Dora Marsden and Harriet Shaw Weaver's *The Egoist*, Margaret Anderson's *Little Review*, Wyndham Lewis and Pound's BLAST, Ford Madox Ford's *English Review* and *transatlantic review*, Robert McAlmon and William Carlos Williams's *Contact*, Harriet Monroe's *Poetry* and T. S. Eliot's *Criterion*, poets and Pound found new venues to publish. For Pound, they were also a financial lifeline since his role as critic/contributor/editor provided a minor income. The phenomenon of the little magazine was not limited to England or the USA. Apollinaire's *Soirées de Paris*, Hugo Ball's *Cabaret Voltaire*, Tristan Tzara's *Dada*, Francis Picabia's *291* and *391*, Man Ray's *TNT*, Kurt Schwitter's *Merz* and Eugene Jolas's *transition* are Continental examples from the early twentieth century that were providing exciting avenues for the avant-garde. Importantly, the little magazines established an international and accessible forum for new work.

Under various titles, Pound played an instrumental role in obtaining and promoting new work for these magazines: variously, he was Foreign Editor, Correspondent, Overseas Editor or, simply, Contributor. Constantly seeking innovative writing, he sent on original or startling material by Robert Frost, H. D., T. S. Eliot, William Carlos Williams, e. e. cummings, Joyce and others. He also constantly looked for support to start his own journal, as his frequent letters to John Quinn, New York patron and collector, attest. And for a short time, he succeeded. His journal, *Exile*, was a semi-successful attempt which, in four issues, did manage to print new work by Louis Zukofsky and Yeats, including the latter's "Sailing to Byzantium" in issue number 3. Too often, however, second-rate writers appeared. Most of the fourth and final issue contained a lengthy political essay by Pound extolling, among other things, Lenin.

BLAST (two issues, June 1914 and July 1915), however, was a particularly noteworthy contribution to the world of the little magazine, its typographical design as important as its radical content. Here was the new Vorticism in material form. The first number of 157 pages, however, was actually delayed because of controversy over several lines in Pound's poem, "Fratres Minores," which were eventually blacked out (the first two and the last lines were the offensive passages: line 1 reads "With minds still hovering above their testicles" [*EPEW*53]). BLAST proclaimed itself the "Review of The Great English Vortex."

The subtitle of the second number was the "War Number," and included two poems by T. S. Eliot. Lewis designed the covers and text with overpowering type and graphics that matched the belligerent manifestos printed in the issues.

Critics reacted indifferently, however, seeing in BLAST merely a water-downed version of Marinetti's Futurist program. One reviewer remarked with hostility that: "Mr. Pound used to be quite interesting when he was a remote passéeist and wrote about Provençal troubadours; but as a revolutionary I would rather have Signor Marinetti, who is at any rate a genuine hustler." Pound, by contrast, seemed like an imitator, more like "a man who is trying to use someone else's coat as a pair of trousers."[6] Such a view saw Vorticism as Futurism in an English bottle.

One of the ironies of Pound's overall project was his choice of the long form for the modern poem. The state of the epic *c.* 1914–17 was questionable. While the Victorians wrote lengthy works like Tennyson's *In Memoriam* or Browning's *The Ring and The Book*, the form was in disfavor during the Edwardian period. Lyrics, odes, sonnets or brief *vers libre* expressions seemed more appropriate and of the moment. The epic appeared clumsy, out-dated and, most importantly, unsuited to the times. Yet Pound, and a series of other modernists, returned to the long form. Hart Crane's *The Bridge* (1930), David Jones's *In Parenthesis* (1937), Zukofsky's *"A"* (1927–8), Williams's *Paterson* (1951), Charles Olson's *Maximus Poems* (1960, 1968, 1975) are notable examples. But it was Pound who felt the epic, in particular, was the genre expansive enough for him to include the historical range and balance he sought. It was also narratively elastic and allowed him to pick moments to elaborate or diminish as Homer did, selecting a single moment, the return of Odysseus, as the focus of the *Odyssey*. Dante may have been Pound's inspiration but the formal structure and purposeful narrative of *The Divine Comedy* did not suit Pound who wanted flexibility and the freedom to leave the ending, if necessary, unfinished. A shorter form could not do that. The Homeric epic was perfect.

Pound was both a part of, and instigator of, these broader poetic changes from the old order to the new. As he redrew the lines of poetry, from the rhetorical and metrically rigid to natural speech and the image, often through the narrative use of a persona, other writers were undertaking similar explorations: Eliot in his many-voiced *The Waste Land* used a panoply of sources and even footnotes; Joyce, in his remarkable *tour de* (literary) *force Ulysses*, drew principally from Homer; H. D., throughout her poetry, relied on the classics and refined Imagist style

Yet modernism had a certain contempt for popular culture which rejected or, more accurately, did not know how to respond to the avant-garde. The complexity of cultural exchange, however, saw modernism try to undo its elitism, although with mixed success. As late as 1930, Pound preferred deluxe editions for his poems. Yet the modernism that emerged between roughly 1912 and 1922, between Imagism and the publication of *Ulysses*, was unusual in its efforts to establish elitist texts, either by accessibility, cost or complexity. Anyone picking up *The Waste Land*, *Ulysses* or *A Draft of XXX Cantos* would be perplexed. The allusive, experimental and fragmented style of the works would make reading difficult. The authors understood the challenges: Eliot responded by adding footnotes, Joyce by drafting a chart of his multi-valenced connections, and Pound by writing more cantos.

Another distinctive aspect of the moderns was the degree of interaction among the main participants. Yeats, for example, put Pound in contact with Joyce; Pound put Eliot in contact with Harriet Monroe and *Poetry*. The so-called "Men of 1914" – a phrase used by Wyndham Lewis in *Blasting and Bombardiering* (1937) to describe Eliot, Pound, Joyce and himself – formed an unusual camaraderie as they stormed the rigid fortress of Victorianism or the newly constructed but unstable house of Edwardian–Georgian art. With Yeats in the lead, the modernists startled; with Pound, they shook things up, sometimes violently.

Of course, the energy of modernism reached the Continent as well. Stravinsky, Kandinsky, Picasso, Stein and Diaghilev were performing, painting or publishing. Imagism was superseding Symbolism, Cubism was trumping Realism. Translation was making internationalism a hallmark of the modernist enterprise with Arthur Symons translating Mallarmé, H. D. translating Greek, Pound translating Cavalcanti and Li Po. Yeats joined this group through his reworking of Gaelic tales and encounter with Noh Theatre, brought to him by Pound during three winters together at Stone Cottage. In his introductory essay, "Certain Noble Plays of Japan," after noting the rejection of naturalistic effects and the essentialness of masks, Yeats comments that the interest is "not in the human form but in the rhythm to which it moves." The triumph of the art is "to express the rhythm in its intensity," something of a program guide to the objective – Eliot would say impersonal – art of the modernists.[7]

From the perspective of 1937, Wyndham Lewis would note that what, indeed, characterized the "Men of 1914," taken as a whole, was their attempt "to get away from romantic art into classical art . . . into the detachment of true literature." His comparison was with Picasso who had terminated the nineteenth-century alliance of painting and natural science, although he also believed that, after the First World War, art had slipped again into "political propaganda and romance." Objectivity had failed but politics was inescapable, as Pound would increasingly trumpet. In 1937, Lewis realized that no one "can help being other than political. We are in politics up to our necks."[8] Nevertheless, the so-called

"High Modernists" sought and sustained a belief in the thing itself. "No ideas but in things," William Carlos Williams would write, telling readers of *Paterson* to move "from mathematics to particulars" (*PAT* 6, 5).

Pound's vigorous attack on complacency and convention was initially literary. He challenged English poetry, especially Victorian, and the entrapment of poets by iambic pentameter. He found textbooks an anathema, teaching a curse. Traditional works like Whitman's *Leaves of Grass* were stultifying and narrow, Pound at one point telling his father "it is impossible to read it without swearing at the author almost continuously" (*SL* 21). Yet Pound also had a generosity of understanding; if energy was present, it was valued. "One doesn't need to like a book or a poem or a picture in order to recognize its artistic vigor," he declared (*LE* 384). His stringent criticism and sharp tone reveal a mind stimulated by literature on three continents: America, Europe and Asia. He promoted a global perspective in his exploration of trans-cultural relations in *Cathay*, the Noh and the Africa of Frobenius. Inter-continental readings which cut through history summarize Pound's approach, expressed in directives, commands and a hortatory style that frequently reduced itself to statements of concision to get readers reading: "Premier principe – REIN that interferes with the words, or with the utmost possible clarity of impact of words on audience . . ." (*SL* 169). Or, in more colorful language, "if you weren't stupider than a mud-duck, you would know that every kick to bad writing is by that much a help for the good" (*SL* 158). The recipient of this advice was William Carlos Williams, but a generation listened.

Pound began to remake his language on or about 1910, recognizing that he had been "obfuscated by the Victorian language" (*LE* 193–4). He needed a new language "to think in." When criticizing his own Rossetti-inflected efforts to translate Guido Cavalcanti, for example, he explained that his mistake was "in taking an English sonnet as the equivalent for a sonnet in Italian" (*LE* 194). The anti-Romantic essays of T. E. Hulme, English philosopher, provided an early guide. In "Romanticism and Classicism," Hulme wrote that "beauty may be in small dry things . . . the great aim is accurate, precise and definite description."[9] By 1912, Pound offered his own corresponding set of rules:

1. Direct treatment of the "thing" whether subjective or objective.
2. To use absolutely no word that does not contribute to the presentation.
3. As regarding rhythm: to compose in the sequence of the musical phrase, not in sequence of a metronome.

(*LE* 3)

What became clear to Pound was the need to "cut direct" and discover, as he would state in his account of the sculptor Gaudier-Brzeska, that "the image is the poet's pigment" (*GB* 19, 86). This also related to Pound's view that one could learn more about poetry by "really knowing and examining a few of the best poems than by meandering about among a great many" (*ABCR* 43). Pound's quest became to "make it new" (LIII/265)

Italy was an important influence on his work, not simply through his living in Venice, Rapallo or Brunnenburg in the Italian Alps, but for its literary ethos. Italian writers and forms defined much of Pound's outlook. Dante, Cavalcanti, Cino and even Petrarch (although he denied the importance of the latter) form a set of shadow images, supported by figures like Sigismundo Malatesta and Mussolini.

Surprisingly, Pound generally did not admire much Italian poetry after Dante, but Giacomo Leopardi, an eighteenth century Italian poet, and Gabriele D'Annunzio, of the twentieth-century, were two exceptions. As Reed Way Dasenbrock shows in *Imitating the Italians*, Leopardi contributed to Pound's sense that, through *canzoni*, he might be able to reinvigorate the lyric tradition. Consequently, he preferred this form to the sonnet.[10] Furthermore, a shared poetry of tension, flux and alteration between the scattered and gathered – the way Petrarch composed his *Canzoniere* – influenced Pound's method of composition and *The Cantos*. Additionally, Pound wrote both prose and poetry in Italian and increasingly admired the country's ability to join culture and politics – Mussolini being one of the major heroes of *The Cantos*. The reasons for his admiration are complex and began with his approval of Mussolini's integration of culture with economics. His later investment in Mussolini had to do with *il Duce*'s ability to resurrect the glory of Malatesta, a desire for economic reforms and a belief that Fascism, rather than liberal democracy, would improve the social order: hero worship resulted.

Indicating Pound's appreciation of Italy and its literary influence is the title of his first book, *A Lume Spento*, taken from Dante's *Purgatorio*. The title of his 1911 volume, borrowed from Petrarch via Leopardi, is *Canzoni*, while the opening of Leopardi's *canzone* "All' Italia" becomes the title of Pound's 1912 prose series, *Patria Mia*. Pound even drew cultural parallels between Italy's apex, the Renaissance, and America, arguing in this series of prose pieces that America was ready for an "American Risorgiomento" or "intellectual awakening" (*PM* 41). Pound frequently drew parallels between the Italian Renaissance and America to stimulate a new, public culture. Even Venice would be remade in America, as he writes in *Patria Mia*: "when Marinetti and his friends shall have succeeded in destroying that ancient city, we will rebuild Venice on the Jersey mud flats and use the same for a tea-shop" (*PM* 33). Appropriately, perhaps, it was Leopardi who used the title *Canzoni* for a collection of his poetry published in 1818 and again in 1824, the source of the title for Pound's 1911 volume. Earlier Italian poets like Cavalcanti, Dante and

Petrarch wrote *canzoni* but Leopardi was the first to use the form as a title for a collection.

The importance of Italy for Pound was reaffirmed through his early study and appreciation of the classical writers which began when he undertook to learn Latin, first at Cheltenham Military Academy and then at the University of Pennsylvania where he took Latin all four terms he was there (1901–3). In fact, he told the poet Donald Hall in 1962 that knowing Latin was the only reason he got into university (*RP* 229). At Penn, he studied Horace, Cicero, Catullus, Tibullus, Propertius and Ovid, Virgil and Lucretius. In 1905–6, when he returned from Hamilton College for a Master's Degree at Penn, he took a Latin Pro-Seminar focusing on Catullus, Martial and Tacitus. His MA degree in "Romanics" (Romance languages) had a Latin minor.[11]

Reading the Latin and later Greek writers had for Pound a clear rationale which he explained in "A Retrospect": "my pawing over the ancients and semi-ancients has been one struggle to find out what has been done, once for all, better than it can ever be done again, and to find out what remains for us to do, and plenty does remain . . ." (*LE* 11). In *Guide to Kulchur* (1938) he continues his respect for the language, suggesting that when it went into decline "there was an as yet uncalculated but very great loss to higher culture in Europe" (*GK* 229). He also admits that he does not regret not having learned Greek. When "a fellow named Spenser recited a long passage of *Iliad* to me, after tennis" that was "worth more than grammar when one was 13 years old" (*GK* 145).

The nineteenth century, Pound believes, will be seen as a "rather blurry, messy sort of a period, a rather sentimentalistic, mannerish sort of a period." It is the classical age that shows the clarity and exactness of the *best* writing has to offer, which he hopes the new poetry will achieve, becoming as "much like granite as it can be." It should be free of "painted adjectives" and become "austere, direct, free from emotional slither" (*LE* 11, 12). Pound believes that poetic progress lies only "in an attempt to approximate classical quantitative metres (NOT to copy them)" (*LE* 13).

Pound remained emphatic on the importance and value of the classics:

> Study the classic books,
> the straight history
> all of it candid.
> (XCIX/731)

The purpose is clear, as he told Margaret Anderson in June 1917:

> You read Catullus to prevent yourself from being poisoned by the lies of pundits; you read Propertius to purge yourself of the greasy sediments of lecture courses on "American Literature," on "English Literature from

Dryden to Addison," you (in extreme cases) read Arnaut Daniel so as
not to be over-awed by a local editor who faces you with a
condemnation in the phrase "paucity of rhyme."   (*SL* 113)

With colorful and direct language, Pound declares that "the classics, 'ancient
and modern,' are precisely the acids to gnaw through the thongs and bulls-
hides with which we are tied by our school-masters . . . they are almost the only
antiseptics against the contagious imbecility of mankind" (*SL* 113; also see *SL*
87). The strength of even the most modern of painters, Picasso, is because he
has largely "chewed through and chewed up a great mass of classicism" which
the "lesser cubists" have not (*SL* 113). Or, as he declared in *Mauberley*, "Better
mendacities / Than the classics in paraphrase!" The classics in their original
language will combat the "tawdry cheapness" of the present (*EPEW* 128, 129).

To underscore his point, he drew on satire. In "Cantico del Sole,"
included in his essay "The Classics 'Escape,'" in *Instigations* (1920), he
writes

> The thought of what America would be like
>   If the Classics had a wide circulation
>   Troubles my sleep.

The very idea of the classics studied in America provides an ironic counter-
weight to the ignorance of their texts. Even the title is satirical referring to his
earlier work "Cantico del Sole," a translation of a text by St. Francis of Assisi
(*EPPT* 572, 127).

Pound wanted to teach readers that the classics counted but it was important
to discriminate, to separate the greater from the lesser. Hence, his didactic
lists and directions that appear throughout his prose: "Catullus, Propertius,
Horace and Ovid are the people who matter. Catullus most. Martial somewhat.
Propertius for beautiful cadence though he uses only one metre. Horace you
will not want for a long time. I doubt if he is of any use save to the Latin scholar"
(*SL* 87). He calls Virgil "a second-rater" in this 1916 letter: "a Tennysonianized
version of Homer. Catullus has the intensity, and Ovid might teach one many
things" (*SL* 87). Their value was incalculable, even in translation. So in 1910, on
a Paris *quai*, Pound chose a Renaissance Latin *Odyssey* to read by Andreas Divus
completed in 1538. His Latin was sound, his Greek spotty. *The Cantos* were
underway, if only conceptually, via a text that had a "grip on detailed actuality"
(*PE* 44). Or as Pound himself wrote, "we proceed by a study of discoveries"
(*LE* 18).

But if Pound understood Latin, his Greek was incomplete; he stated in a
1916 letter that he prized Greek "more for the movement of the words, rhythm,
perhaps than for anything else" (*SL* 91). Nevertheless in 1918–19, he published

four articles on translations of Homer, reprinted as "Translators of Greek: Early Translators of Homer" in *Instigations* (1920) which opens with a lament on the decline of the classics: "The dilection of Greek poets has waned during the last pestilent century, and this decline has, I think, kept pace with a decline in the use of Latin cribs to Greek authors. The classics have more and more become a baton exclusively for the cudgeling of schoolboys, and less and less a diversion for the mature" (*LE* 249).

Throughout his critical and poetic writings, the classics loom large. A list of the key authors, in addition to Homer, would include Catullus, Sappho, Propertius, Horace (responsible for more than half the bad poetry written in English, he asserts), Ovid and dubious cases like Virgil and Petrarch. The latter, he writes, "refines but deenergizes" (in *SR* 166). Throughout his essays and studies like the *ABC of Reading*, it is the classics that Pound upholds. And the appeal of Latin he makes explicit first in one of his earliest published poems, "To the Raphaelite Latinists" (1908), and then throughout his prose where he repeatedly asserts the internationalism of the language: "As distinct from the classic tradition, Latin had belonged to all Europe" (*ABCR* 132).

In "How to Read," Pound outlines a program of study in order to form sound judgments. The authors are characteristically few: Homer, Sappho, Catullus, Ovid, Propertius and Horace, in limited dosages. As always, Pound is opinionated and clear:

> I am chucking out Pindar, and Virgil, without the slightest
> compunction. I do not suggest a "course" in Greek or Latin literature, I
> name a few isolated writers; five or six pages of Sappho. One can throw
> out at least one-third of Ovid. That is to say, I am omitting the authors
> who can teach us no new or no more effective method of "charging
> words."   (*LE* 28)

A newly discovered Sapphic fragment directly inspired Pound's 1916 poem "Papyrus." The poem is a meditation on lyric desire importantly making the fragment the aesthetic ideal, foreshadowing Pound's later emphasis on "gists and piths." It is the literary representation of a literally fragmented text, with meaning deferred, time suspended. The entire poem reads

> Spring . . .
> Too long . . .
> Gongula . . .

The last word names a disciple and possible lover of Sappho (*EPPT* 289)

Although Pound's tastes changed, his allegiance to the classical writers who formulated his poetic outlook did not: Homer, Sappho, Catullus, Propertius,

Ovid, plus classical mythology, remained. The classical poets, especially Homer and Propertius, and their use of masks, made it possible for Pound to find his own voice. Schematically, one might see Catullus shaping Pound's lyric mode, Propertius the dramatic, and Ovid the epic. The intensity of Catullus, the dramatic masks of Propertius and the metamorphic dimension of Ovid all contributed to Pound's multiple voices. Collectively, they aided him in choosing a form essentially rejected by the public: the epic.

The presence of the long poem in the Victorian period was evident in the work of Tennyson, through his elegy *In Memoriam*, and Clough, in his lively verse narrative/travelogue, *Amours de Voyage*, a set of verse epistles. It was Browning, however, who undertook the long poem with determination and success, notably in *Sordello* (1840) and *The Ring and the Book* (1868). The former Pound found intriguing partly because Browning based the lengthy work on the thirteenth-century Italian troubadour who was in service to Charles of Anjou. Dante cites him in *Purgatorio* VII. For Pound, the poem, with its elliptical syntax, bookish diction, condensed narrative and discursive interludes, set an experimental pattern he would later follow. And despite Victorian claims that the poem was obscure and difficult, Pound found it fascinating ever since he first read it at Hamilton College. Years later in the *ABC of Reading*, he would quote a substantial passage, claiming that only "Victorian half-wits" would think the poem obscure (*ABCR* 191).

What Pound praises in *Sordello* is its "lucidity of sound" which few works in English possess, as well as a certain clarity of narrative outline "without clog and *verbal* impediment" (*ABCR* 191). One would have to go back to Dante for a parallel. The "beauty" of the work is that it "makes the mental image more definite. The author is not hunting about for large, high-sounding words." As in the case with Arthur Golding (translator of Ovid), he concludes that one must read *Sordello* "as prose, pausing for the sense and not hammering the line-terminations" (*ABCR* 191).

Yet with Homer and Dante as models, Pound felt the epic form – revised – could be the only form that could contain the multidimensional narrative he would construct. Ironically, it is Virgil rather than any other of his classical heroes that might lead the way. But he stands as a kind of anti-mask for Pound's work, criticized for his rhetoric and negative influence on Milton but at the same time difficult to overlook because of the *Aeneid* and the voyage of his hero. Pound's claim in "The Renaissance" (1914) – "not Virgil, especially not the Aeneid, where he has no story worth telling, no sense of personality" – would be tempered by the end of his career when Pound effected a sort of reconciliation with the poet. Athens not Rome, would remain the literary *locus classicus* for Pound.

Pound's choice of the epic form for *The Cantos* was a sign of his lasting homage to the classics and how such forms live, change and grow. It was also large, expansive and capable of containing the wealth of reference, allusion and material he began to interpolate. It also allowed, because of its expansiveness, for a certain opaque texture, noted on the simplest level by his leaving many of the foreign languages untranslated. The epic also permitted, if not encouraged, the spatial organization of text which the late cantos took full advantage of. The individual form of each canto also allowed Pound maximum discontinuity, both within separate units and lines, and from canto to canto. The epic was elastic.

Pound's sense of an epic, however, differed from that of his classical predecessors. His conception of it married the dramatic monologue with a select group of heroes, historical and modern, whom he wanted to present epically: Malatesta, Jefferson, John Adams, Confucius, Mussolini. No single hero, he realized, could carry his poem or reflect his age. The luxury of return would probably not be available as his long poem continued; he most likely would not be able to bring his hero home. In the end, he would be unable to sustain the circular journey of Odysseus who returns to Ithaca; rather, Pound would continue the historically linear narrative of Aeneas presented by Ovid, a figure Pound both accepts and rejects. In 1938 in *Guide to Kulchur* Pound writes that, from decade to decade, he keeps repeating that Ovid "is one of the most interesting of all enigmas" (*LE* 215; *GK* 272). Pound, it seems, rejected Ovid precisely because of his epic success, finding emotion, irony and the polytheism he admired in other Latin poets.

In *The Spirit of Romance*, however, Pound admits that he found the urbane and questioning Ovid compelling. In a skeptical age longing for the definite, Ovid makes the supernatural plausible. His gods are humanized, his heroes natural. In his poetry, most importantly, the "mood, the play is everything; the facts are nothing. Ovid, before Browning, raises the dead and dissects their mental processes" (*SR* 16). In many ways this outlines the process of *The Cantos* which a passage in *Guide to Kulchur* reaffirms when Pound asserts that there is great truth in Ovid "and in the subject matter of Ovid's long poem and that only in this form could it be registered" (*GK* 299). Earlier, in a letter of 1922, he avows that the writings of Confucius and Ovid's *Metamorphoses* are "the only safe guides in religion" and that the *Metamorphoses* is a "sacred book" (*SL* 183).

Ovid is an enigma for Pound because he is a political and religious skeptic who considers the gods merely convenient, portraying them as human beings. Yet Ovid became a guide to the structure of *The Cantos* on various levels. When he wrote to his father in 1917 admitting that the "whole damn poem is rather obscure, especially in fragments," Pound also hopes for a "'magic moment' or moment of metamorphosis, bust thru from quotidien into 'divine or permanent world.' Gods, etc." alluding to Ovid (*SL* 210). Ovid's importance for Pound lay in the human needs, desires and weaknesses of his gods. Or, as he writes in *Mauberley*, mocking a line in Pindar's second Olympian, "What god, man, or hero / Shall I place a tin wreath upon!" (*EPEW* 129). Significantly, most of Canto IV consists of myths and legends, resembling a book of the *Metamorphoses* as one myth leads to another. Where Pound digresses from Ovid is in the absence of a sequential narrative.

Ovid hovers about *The Cantos* as Pound attempts, but is unable, to unite Ovidian metamorphosis with neo-Platonic philosophy, and Confucian ideology with social order: "I am not a demigod, / I cannot make it cohere" (CXVI/816). Other classical figures – Plautinus, Heraclitus and Sophocles – were important to Pound but the Latin poets above all, with Homer, remain the central classical figures who propel his writing forward as he looked back to their work. A short statement from "Credo" (1930) restates his attachment and its union with his aesthetic: "Having a strong disbelief in abstract and general statements as a means of conveying one's thoughts to others, I have for a number of years answered such questions by telling the enquirer to read Confucius and Ovid" (*SP* 53). Importantly, Pound's sense of literary culture was inclusive, although the classics, while important, were not necessarily privileged. They were to be integrated with world literature and become part of modern times.

Affiliated with Pound's focus on the classics was translation – its status, at the time he began to write, dismal at best; its practice, inaccurate at worst. As a comparatist, he notes that histories of Spanish and Italian literature always consider translators. Histories of English literature do not ("I suppose it is inferiority complex") – yet "some of the best books in English are translations" (*LE* 34). Following the Anglo-Saxon period, he explains in *How to Read*, "English literature lives on translation; every new exuberance, every new heave is stimulated by translation, every allegedly great age is an age of translations" (*LE* 34–5). Naturally, he, too, undertook translations, which had varying success.

Pound essentially understood translation as a creative endeavor. The spirit, not the literal word, was important for him, contrary to Victorian translators who preferred literalized and versified meter. Pound found this an anathema. His attitude might be best expressed in Alfred's "Preface" to *his* translation of Pope Gregory's *Cura pastoralis* – "Here one can still see their track, but we cannot follow their footsteps" – which gave Pound license to make his translations freer. Notable Victorian translations such as Cary's Dante or William Morris's Icelandic sagas or Philip Stanhope Worsley's Spenserian *Odyssey* remained enclosed, limited and unpoetic. Fitzgerald's *Rubaiyat* was closer to his own goals which were the opposite of A. E. Housman's, who sought literal language. For Pound, the Greek, Latin, Chinese or Provençal poem was "a hypothesis for something new," Pound fashioning a new form "similar in effect to that of the original" (*PT* 9). To be a translator is to be a poet for Pound, who understood the process as the acculturation of texts from one language and period to another. However, reaction to such creativity, as marked by the appearance of his four translated stanzas of "Propertius" in *Poetry* of 1917, was virulent. Classicists were offended, although readers pleased.

Pound's idea about translation was to bring emotion into focus, while remaining true to the source text. Pound sought to render not the words of the original but the sensibility or thing identified, which might be seafaring as in "The Seafarer" or the sensibility accompanying the Tuscan anatomy of love as in "Cino." Being faithful to the original sequence of images, rhythm and tone, although not the words, is also part of Pound's pattern. Homage is perhaps the accurate term for what Pound undertakes, the result more the construction of personae than a translation in any literal sense.

Pound's "translations" ranged widely from Latin, Provençal, French, Italian, Anglo-Saxon, and Chinese to Greek. *Cathay* is a high point as Pound matches delicacy with imagery. Confucius is a cornerstone, especially in Pound's translation of *The Unwobbling Pivot* and the *Analects*. The practice is reciprocal, as Hugh Kenner noted. Confucius, after twenty-four centuries, "stirs Pound to speech; Pound after twenty-four centuries lends Confucius his voice" (*PT* 14).

Pound's understanding of Chinese was at best incomplete. He never formally studied the language and is today considered to have misread much of the material. His main study of the Chinese classics occurred in the mid-1930s, his main tools several Chinese–English dictionaries. But his lexical labors did not permit him to read widely in Confucian scholarship, nor to obtain a sound grasp of the language. For his main project of translating Confucius, he relied on a French translation by Guillaume Pauthier and a bi-lingual translation by James Legge. In August 1937, he went on a retreat to concentrate on his Chinese texts, taking the Legge crib with him – although when he disagreed with it, he had little to go on. Legge, ex-missionary to China and Oxford's first Professor of Chinese (1876), had an important effect on Pound, although the former, like Pauthier, made mistakes.[12] But Pound's insufficient knowledge of Chinese, compounded by his intuitive approach, generated his own semantic and grammatical errors in his readings, later gathered and published in 1951 as *Confucian Analects*. He published an earlier summary of the text in *Confucius. Digest of the Analects* (1937), reprinted in *Guide to Kulchur* (15–21).

With the classics on one side of the world and Confucius on the other, it is easy to overlook Pound's persistent identification with America. While the classical world and Confucius were the two complementary forces that united his own poetic, drawing on Italian, French, English and Chinese sources, America remained the fulcrum. In numerous ways *The Cantos* is an American poem with its focus on the building of the Republic, the discussion of core documents like the Constitution and the focus on such major figures as Jefferson and John Adams. American history is fundamental to the theme and structure of the poem.

But Pound was also relentlessly critical of America and its poets – "nine out of every ten Americans have sold their souls for a quotation" – yet he still felt an allegiance that would remain throughout his life (*PM* 23). He proudly possessed "a Plymouth-rock conscience," marked by honesty and directness (*SL* 12). He believed in an "American Risorgimento" and proudly, even in England, promoted the work of Americans: Robert Frost, H. D. and, of course, T. S. Eliot (*SL* 10). It's strong, objective writing, he remarks about H. D.'s work, containing "no slither; direct – no excessive use of adjectives, no metaphors that won't permit examination." In colloquial American language, he says "it's straight talk, straight as the Greek!" (*SL* 11). The connection is notable: American frankness equals Greek directness.

Pound continuously identified himself as an American, rhetorically challenging Williams when he asked "wot bloody kind of author are you save Amurkun (same as me)?" A moment later he stated: "if you had any confidence in America you wouldn't be so touchy about it" (*SL* 123). He then lit into Williams, challenging his American pedigree when he had never been "west of Upper Darby": "Would Harriet [Monroe] with the swirl of the prairie wind in her underwear, or the virile Sandburg recognize you, an effete Easterner as a REAL American? INCONCEIVABLE!!!!" (*SL* 124). By contrast, Pound had "the virus, the bacillus of the land in my blood, for nearly three bleating centuries." Furthermore, opacity saved Williams's poems but "opacity is NOT an American quality. Fizz, swish, gabble of verbiage, these are echt Amerikanisch" (*SL* 124). What he demanded of Williams is more "robustezza." If he didn't start to show it in his work, Pound threatened to "come over to Rutherford, [N. J.] and have at you, *coram*, in person" (*SL* 124).

Pound's American identity never wavered as he wrote from Rapallo in 1939: "Am I American? Yes, and buggar the present state of the country, the utter betrayal of the American Constitution" (*SL* 322). And then, considering the cultural future of the country, he makes absolutely clear that Americans need to have American authors. What is required, he emphasizes, is a book of sixty or eighty pages "of *selections* of gists of the writings of Adams, Jefferson, Van

Buren, Jackson, Johnson," fundamental American voices accessible to all (*SL* 325).

Betrayal of the US Constitution emerges as a theme of Pound's in the 1940s, repeated in his radio broadcasts for Mussolini's Fascist government directed at the United States. Over and over again, Pound defends the Constitution and indicts the government for violating its laws. In *The Cantos*, he also repeatedly cites the making of the Constitution as a crucial step in establishing an American identity. For Pound, the Constitution defines the American character, the government and his "work." Pound never doubted he was a patriot, his job to be the voice of America before it entered the morass of war. He, therefore, found his indictment for treason by a US Grand Jury unbelievable.

American writers, however, were less defensible. Whitman, for example, was "a hard nutt" with *Leaves of Grass* the book to face. In a 1909 essay, "What I Feel About Walt Whitman," Pound at first wants to Europeanize him, "to drive Whitman into the old world. I sledge, he drill – and to scourge America with all the old beauty . . . and with a thousand thongs from Homer to Yeats, from Theocritus to Marcel Schwob" (*SP* 116). Admiration and recognition balance his antagonism, however, and realization that he was probably more like Whitman than Cavalcanti. "A Pact," printed in *Poetry* in 1913, announces a truce, recognizing that Whitman broke new poetic ground and that "we have one sap and one root – / Let there be commerce between us" (*EPEW* 74). In *Patria Mia*, Pound ambivalently added that "Whitman was not an artist, but a reflex, the first honest reflex, in an age of papier-mâché letters" (*PM* 38). But he recognizes and accepts that "mentally I am a Walt Whitman who has learned to wear a collar and a dress shirt" and that Whitman is to his country what Dante is to Italy, concluding that one must pay more attention to "the artistry of the man" (*SP* 115, 116). With James and Whistler, Pound added Whitman to his list of formative American artists.

Pound's love of America also came through, although radicalized and racialized, in his radio broadcasts during the Second World War. Throughout the more than 120 recorded transmissions, he constantly expressed his attachment to America, while condemning Roosevelt, the decision to fight and the control of the country by powerful interest groups. He repeatedly lamented the demise of the country: "Here lies America, she died of the romance of luxury" (*EPS* 62). America, he repeats, has receded and needs to revivify itself (*EPS* 223). Part of what Pound did in maintaining his American identity in Europe was to redefine American culture by showing how in many ways it was borderless. Henry Adams, Whistler, James, Wharton, Eliot, Stein, Hemingway, Fitzgerald and, of course, Pound made it clear that a native American aesthetic was not separate from, but absorbed in, its European origins. In Pound's case, this occurred through his engagement with the cultures of England, France, Italy and even China, all embedded in *The Cantos*. He was, furthermore, bringing the classics to bear on American writing, fashioning an American voice, always an American voice, through the masks of a Homer, Catullus or Propertius.

Distorting perspective through juxtaposition, whether through image or language, also placed Pound within the scope of the Surrealists, Dadaists and even Constructivists. Their experimentation and his innovation meshed as he manipulated blocks of history or documents to create a flat surface, as in Cubist or early Dada collage, where fragmented images and bits of narrative are brought into collision. Subordinating the referential to the sequential or spatial became common practice for Pound and these modern artists, who decompose rather than recreate history. But, like Eliot and Joyce, Pound mastered past conventions before undertaking new ones. What he undertook – revitalizing language, restructuring the long poem, and instructing a culture on its future via its past – was happening throughout Europe, expressed by an aesthetic that challenged conventions through multiple perspectives, a Bergsonian sense of simultaneity and the creation of verbal collage where terms like past and present seem irrelevant. But his treatment of fragmentation and anti-mimetic bias reflected developments in other modernist forms as well, especially in art, music and prose fiction. Pound, however, made it stick, partly because his major work, *The Cantos*, continued over such a long period, remaining essentially unfinished at his death. Pound's artistic career, from the late Victorian to the Post-modern age, was lengthy. He knew both Hardy and Allen Ginsberg.

Chapter 3

Works

Poetry to 1920

> The poet's job is to *define* and yet again define till the detail of surface is in accord with the root in justice.
>
> Pound, 1935 (*SL* 277)

Pound's early work consists of rewriting and making new earlier forms of poetic expression. The sestina, Provençal lyric and dramatic monologue are three particular examples of his effort to unite detail and justice, form and ethics. He replaced Swinburne's arabesques with Arnaut Daniel's precision, Pre-Raphaelite elaborations with Imagism's exactness, the "Blaze of color intermingled" with the detail of "Green arsenic smeared on an egg-white cloth" (*CEP* 261; *EPEW* 84). Pound writes in color, with definiteness, elaborating a statement by the American photographer Paul Outerbridge (1896–1958) who said "with black and white you can suggest, but with colour you have to be certain, absolutely certain."[1] In his poetry and criticism, Pound was, without a doubt, certain.

Pound's encounter with the exactness of Chinese poetry at the time he was working out his poetic practice, expressed through Imagism (*c.* 1912), and then through his re-vision of Chinese poetry in *Cathay* (1915), reaffirmed his drive toward precision. His editing and publishing Fenollosa's "The Chinese Written Character as a Medium for Poetry" (1919) further clarified this poetic which Dante, Arnaut Daniel, the Provençal poets and the Chinese had advanced. His early, lyrical work, with overtones of Romanticism and the Pre-Raphaelites, culminates in the satiric and multi-voiced "Homage to Sextus Propertius" (1919) and *Hugh Selwyn Mauberley* (1920). At the same time, he was formulating the structure and content of his long, expansive work that lacked a title more specific than *The Cantos*, which first began to appear in *Poetry* in 1917, the final volume published in 1969.

Personae, or the search for a persona, might characterize Pound's early quest; epic might summarize his later pursuit in a work of 117 cantos. But his career was never simple, his poetic path never straight. As he summarizes in "Notes for CXVII et seq.," "I have tried to write Paradise" but "I lost my center / fighting the world" (CXVII/822). However, Pound never questioned the value of poetry in shaping the world.

Pound's earliest writing, *Hilda's Book*, stitched together (quite literally: it was a handmade book) a collection of effusive lyrics for Hilda Doolittle, his early Philadelphia love, later renamed by him H. D. They display tradition not originality and have lines like "I pray thee love these wildered words of mine: / Tho I be weak, is beauty always strong" (*EPPT* 3). Titles are in Italian, French, Latin and English, suggesting an arch use of tradition. *A Lume Spento*, Pound's first published book (Venice, 1908) carried on the early tradition of inherited verse, with some new material which he began to write in Crawfordsville, Indiana, during his short tenure as a professor of Romance languages at Wabash College. Reflecting a lifetime interest in the production of his books, Pound personally supervised the printing of *A Lume Spento* on paper remaindered from a history of the church (*EPM* 163).

Pound's early poetry was rooted in emotion, a kind of late Victorian, Pre-Raphaelite world of color and imagery focusing on beauty. But like Tennyson, Browning and even Yeats, he began to attribute this emotion to another speaker, a persona. The term originated in the habit of Roman actors wearing clay masks, the Latin for mask being *persona*, originating in a verb meaning to "sound through." In the classical period, the term also meant character. Appropriately, Pound titled his first London volume, *Personae* (1909). Essentially, from his study of early Romance literatures, Pound imitated the troubadour origins of modern lyric poetry and returned to a personalized history; as he writes at the end of "Provincia Deserta," "I have thought of them living." His eclectic taste united twelfth-century Provence, eighth-century China and first-century Rome. From the last, he developed a set of poems on modern life that were epigrammatic and imagistic, often found inset in longer works like "Homage to Sextus Propertius" and *Mauberley*. Manifestoes such as "A Pact" also appeared, a poetic statement of his rough bond with Whitman (*EPEW* 74). But in his effort to make poetry new, he knew he must first learn from the past, as he noted in 1915: "the first step of a renaissance, or awakening, is the importation of models for painting, sculpture or writing . . . we must learn what we can from the past" – to understand its excellence and see the inadequacies of the present (*LE* 214, 219).

For Pound the key to his poetry is often his prose, as *The Spirit of Romance* (1910), initially a set of lectures he gave in London on Romance literature, illustrates. The book records his absorption with Italian poets and Provençal troubadours whose works his poetry imitated. It also shows Pound freeing himself from the pedantics of nineteenth-century philology in addressing the nature of Romance literature, attempting as well a link between poetry and science. In the book, for example, he defines poetry as "a sort of inspired mathematics, which gives us equations, not for abstract figures . . . but equations for the human emotions" (*SR* 14). He also repeats his desire to define, to know things and feelings exactly, which he would reiterate in the *ABC of Reading* (1934).

Restraint is another quality of his work which he finds in the poetry of Dante and Arnaut Daniel. Provençal poetry becomes Pound's ideal, not only in terms of its exact imagery and tone but in its use of metrics. It was made to sing, and throughout his writing career *melopeia*, as he would later term it, and music would be fundamental. His involvement with Olga Rudge, violinist, and George Antheil, composer, is another expression of the importance of music in his writing. The composition of his opera *Le Testament de Villon* (performed in Paris, 1926) further deepened his absorption with music.

A set of his early poems imitates the Provençal style, culturally and poetically. "Near Perigord" and "Cino" are two clear examples. The first, appearing in *Poetry* in 1915, is a dramatic rendering by Bertran de Born, a twelfth-century troubadour, to a woman he loves who is the captive of another. The narrator alternates between allusion and action:

> Take the whole man, and ravel out the story.
> He loved this lady in castle Montagnac?
> The castle flanked him – he had need of it
> (*EPEW* 92)

Pound explores the link between love and politics, showing how de Born uses poetry to subvert the power of his enemies through praise of the women he admired. Throughout, the narrator self-consciously comments on his process, at one point announcing, "End fact. Try fiction" (*EPEW* 94). "Near Perigord" is assured and confident, as Pound fashions a narrative out of "a shifting change, / A broken bundle of mirrors" (*EPEW* 97). "Cino" is earlier (1908) but exhibits the same power through the voice of the troubadour, Cino. It opens with

> Bah! I have sung women in three cities,
> But it is all the same;
> And I will sing of the sun.   (*EPEW* 4)

Yet throughout these poems which emphasize history and action, Pound maintains an element of paganism, writing that "a light from Eleusis [location of Greek fertility ceremonies] persisted through the middle ages and set beauty to the song of Provence and of Italy" (*SP* 53).

Pound moved to Italy from Provence in his study, believing that the *dolce stil nuovo* poetry of the late thirteenth century – Dante, Cavalcanti, Cino da Pistoia – descended from Provençal verse. Shakespeare may be suggestive but Dante is definite, he writes in *The Spirit of Romance*. Villon emerges as another important figure and suddenly Pound's early European idols are evident. But his English influences are equally clear: Rossetti, Browning, Swinburne and the Anglo-Saxon poets. He alternately found their work wonderful and awful and responded to it in varying ways. Supplemented by Whitman, Noh drama and Chinese poetry, he soon found his own voice and style, a blend of American idioms and exactness: use "no word that does not contribute to the presentation," he proclaims in his *Literary Essays* (3). The concrete not the abstract, the definite not the general, was his mantra.

Accompanying Pound's early, neo-Victorian, Arnoldian view of "culture" is an element of agitation: "A sound poetic training is nothing more than the science of being discontented"; "Great art does not depend upon comfort"; "good art, goes against the grain of contemporary taste" (*LE* 216, 221, 223). This restlessness has a rebellious streak, opposing the conventional and the accepted as new heroes emerge in the construction of the "clean palette": Dante, Villon, Arnaut Daniel, Anglo-Saxon poetry and the Chinese, as he outlines in "The Renaissance" (1915). Overthrow of "pretentious and decorated verse," as well as poetry of a "formal verbalism" is the new goal which his own poetry increasingly expressed (*LE* 216).

A passage from Section V of "Und Drang" identifies a new, modern view, a mixture of disillusionment and hope:

> How our modernity,
> Nerve-wracked and broken, turns
> Against time's way and all the way of things,
> Crying with weak and egoistic cries!
>
> (*EPPT* 167)

The "restless will," however, seeks "new moods of life / New permutations" and in Section VI of the poem he glances at what lies ahead when he partially glimpses a face of one he admires:

> The whole face
> Was nothing like you, yet that image cut
> Sheer through the moment.
>
> (*EPPT* 167)

How to "cut / Sheer through the moment" is what Pound pursues and then discovers through Imagism, his first formal step in the renaissance he seeks.

Pound, as a poet, was not above repudiating earlier work that he once accepted as poetry, defending his own efforts in his search to renew old forms through new voices. In "Salutation the Second," for example, which appeared in *Lustra* (1916), he comments that although his early books were "twenty years behind the times," they nevertheless stand "with nothing archaic about them." With pleasure he tells them to "go and dance shamelessly" to "greet the grave and the stodgy, / Salute them with your thumbs at your noses." More directly, he writes: "Dance and make people blush, / Dance the dance of the phallus." His cry is enthusiastic: "rejuvenate things!" (*EPPT* 266). However, his praise is ironic because Elkin Mathews published what Pound called a "castrato" edition, removing several poems from *Lustra*. Omitted texts included "The Temperaments," "Ancient Music" and "Pagani's, November 8." A second impression of the book saw nine further poems removed, including "Salutation the Second." Mathews likely did this because of the suppression of D. H. Lawrence's *The Rainbow* in 1915 and from fear that Pound's language might be offensive. Pound, however, long opposed censorship, writing angrily in 1916 in *The Egoist* in opposition to the American censorship of Theodore Dreiser's novel *The Genius*.

Pound's hard-edged modernity and flinty rejection of his immediate but *not* classical or Provençal predecessors appeared in early work like "Sestina Altaforte" (1909). Pound provided an interesting record of this particular poem, outlining its writing in "How I Began" (1913). Composed of seven stanzas plus an epigraph, it is based on a war song by Bertran de Born. Pound echoes the repetitive structure of the original by using the sestina form that rotates a set of six six-line stanzas and a three-line *envoi*. Repeated line endings unite the pattern. The sestina offered to Pound what he calls in his article "the curious involution and recurrence of form." He wrote the first strophe of the poem and then went "to the British Museum to make sure of the right order of the permutations . . . I did the rest of the poem at a sitting" (*EPEW* 214). This was the first poem Pound published in England.

Pound's first public reading of the poem was as memorable as it was voluble. It occurred at the Tour Eiffel restaurant in Soho at a meeting of the Poets' Club in April 1909. The reading was so emphatic that spoons jumped on the table and a screen had to be placed around the gathering to prevent a public disturbance. He also "opened fire" with the poem for Gaudier-Brzeska, adding that "I think it was the 'Altaforte' that convinced him that I would do to be sculpted" (*GB* 43).

Following a headnote introducing Bertran de Born as presented by Dante, Pound begins emphatically with a vigorous, distinctive voice filled with determination and energy, not unlike Pound's own. The poem goes on to describe nature in a violent manner as he almost allegorically calls out for the renewal of battle: "Hell grant soon we hear again the swords clash!" (*EPEW* 17). Peace is "womanish"; it is time for action: "Hell blot black for alway the thought 'Peace!'" (*EPEW* 18).

"Sestina: Altaforte" appeared in *Exultations* (1909), a volume that shows, in a number of additional works, Pound's renewal of poetic energy through his engagement with Provençal verse. "Piere Vidal Old," "Ballade of the Goodly Fere" and "Histrion" illustrate his new direction. The old style, that of the ballad, albas, madrigals or *tenzoni*, is gone. In their place are Pound's re-invigorated dramatic monologues or social critiques, as in "Aux Belles de Londres" which begins with "I am aweary with the utter and beautiful weariness / And with the ultimate wisdom and with things terrene," the diction of "aweary" and "terrene" creating an interlaced geography between past traditions and new visions (*EPPT* 117). The five-line poem creates a lament for a passing beauty, that is decadent in its tone at the same time that it anticipates a new energy. Pound is in transition in this volume, drawn to new uses of the dramatic monologue's structure but filling the form with traditional content as in "Laudantes Decem Pulchritudinis Johannae Templi" (translating the corrupt Latin, it reads "Ten [Stanzas] Praising the Temple of Giovanna's Beauty") and "Alba Innominata," the "alba" a Provençal song form lamenting the arrival of dawn and separation of lovers. His use of the sonnet form for "Portrait, from La Mère Inconnue" again demonstrates his metamorphic treatment of older genres. This is Provence and even Italy, yet with a modern slant.

Pound was working toward, and discovering, the use of the persona, an extension of the dramatic monologue. "Piere Vidal Old," also in *Exultations*, demonstrates the new tone. It opens, again, directly:

> When I but think upon the great dead days
> And turn my mind upon that splendid madness,
> Lo! I do curse my strength
> And blame the sun his gladness. (*EPEW* 19)

The disgruntled speaker longs for disruption, war. The "Ballade of the Goodly Fere" sustains this directness of voice which "Sestina: Altaforte," the second poem in the volume, introduced. In many ways, *Exultations* is a continuation of

Personae, his 1909 volume, which was an augmented version of *A Quinzane for this Yule* originally published by Pound (at his expense) in 1908. He would re-use the title *Personae* for an expanded volume in 1926 subtitled "The Collected Poems of Ezra Pound," which includes most of his major and minor work up to that date. It contains a frontispiece drawing of Pound by Gaudier-Brzeska and stands as a summary volume of Pound's work as he continued, energetically, to write *The Cantos*. (*A Draft of XVI Cantos* appeared the year before.) The 231-page *Personae*, however, is less an anthology of his work than a poetic summing-up and manifesto of his working technique.

The importance of the persona as a device for Pound cannot be overstated because, by evoking the voice of another, Pound was able to express both the dramatic and the lyric. He was able to cast off "as it were, complete masks of the self in each poem" (*GB* 85). Strong emotion could now be dramatically expressed in his work because it was another who expressed it; the actual poet could hide. In this manner, Pound could be both modern and not modern, adapting both a Provençal method and late nineteenth-century practice to his contemporary concerns. *Hugh Selwyn Mauberley* (1920), with its varied voices and forms, demonstrates this fully. Pound's diction, however, occasionally exposes his still dated use of language, in which sensibility exceeds its object. But he was finding his way, as he explained in "Vorticism" (1914): "In the 'search for oneself,' . . . one gropes, one finds some seeming verity . . . I began this search for the real in a book called *Personae* casting off, as it were, complete masks of the self in each poem. I continued in a long series of translations, which were but more elaborate masks" (*EPEW* 282). The reference here is likely to his edition of the *Sonnets and Ballate of Guido Cavalcanti* (1912) and his work at the time on Fenollosa's Chinese translations, to appear in 1915 as Pound's *Cathay*. But masks of the self are the core of *Personae*, the title acknowledging Browning's *Dramatis Personae* of 1864.

In 1912, Pound published *Ripostes*, a volume dedicated to William Carlos Williams and with a humorous misprint in the list of Pound's books, "Personal" appearing as the incorrect title for "Persona." The text is relatively undistinguished, with tributes to Swinburne; "Salve Pontifex" and "Silet" echoing the opening of a Keats sonnet. "Portrait d'une Femme" is a critique of London and its emptying effect on a young woman, culture contributing only "Strange spars of knowledge and dimmed wares of price" (*EPEW* 45). Curiously, the poem was rejected by the *North American Review* in January 1912 because Pound had used the letter "r" three times in the first line causing difficulty with pronunciation. This convinced Pound that American editors chose work only according to fixed formulas. The line reads "Your mind and you are our Sargasso Sea" (*EPEW* 45).

The exceptional poem in *Ripostes* is "The Seafarer," Pound's version of the Anglo-Saxon poem. The choice at first seems unexpected, since Pound's focus was on Romance languages of southern Europe. But his interest in the meter, the Anglo-Saxon verse-line with its heave in the middle of two alliteratively combined rhythms, is what reinforces his metric revolution and allows him to speak of the half-line rather than the line. He would include "The Seafarer" in *Cathay* because he believed it was the only English poem equal to Li Po's "The Exile's Letter." Both works also contain direct address and complete self-exposure.

Pound's version of "The Seafarer," however, is extremely inaccurate. Misunderstandings abound, as when he translates *stearn* (a seabird) for the stern of a ship; *byrig* (towns) for berries; or *thurb* (through or in) for *thruh* (tomb). The original also acknowledges Christianity but Pound eliminates any such references – a necessary act, perhaps, if he wanted to create a poet who would expose himself with the same unconcern for opinion as Li Po in "The Exile's Letter." But Pound replaces Christian values with something almost barbaric, altering the very nature of the poem, making malice a source of renown, as Li Po did by his drunkenness and attraction to concubines. What Pound creates in "The Seafarer" is a work with a voice that "sings of things as they are," as he had written of Villon (*SR* 171).

The poem extends other voyage poems by Pound, notably "At the Heart o' Me," sung by an unnamed Anglo-Saxon sailor, and "Guido Invites You Thus," where Cavalcanti answers a sonnet by Dante in which a voyage is proposed. The voyage motif of "The Seafarer" also anticipates the more major works structured around Odysseus and his voyage seen in *Mauberley* and *The Cantos*. In his translation of "The Seafarer," however, Pound shocks the reader by eliminating Christian references, removing the last nine lines which contain moral instruction and a hymn to God. He also alters a passage where men are advised to combat the malice of devils and misreads *engles* (angels) as angles. Devils and angels disappear in the work.

Pound's note when the poem appeared in the *New Age* begins with "the text of this poem is rather confused" and summarizes the unclear provenance of the text.[2] He then gives the work a secular vitality, with the unexpected appearance of the philistine middle class, mis-translating *beorn* (man, warrior) as "Burgher":

> This he little believes, who aye in winsome life
> Abides 'mid burghers some heavy business,
> Wealthy and wine-flushed, how I wary oft
> Must bide above brine.   (*EPEW* 49)

What the poem stresses is the solitary and harsh experience of the seafaring Anglo-Saxon. He has known "many a care's hold / And dire sea-surge" spent alone in the night. Listen to my sorrows at sea, he asks:

> List how I, care-wretched, on ice-cold sea,
> Weathered the winter, wretched outcast
> Deprived of my kinsmen   (*EPEW* 48)

Isolation, deprivation and danger characterize his experience, where the sound of sea fowls became for him laughter. Those on land and satisfied know little of such danger, says the speaker, yet he has chosen the heroic route and to go alone, yet he remains pulled to home. But the present, he knows, is empty:

> Days little durable,
> And all arrogance of earthen riches,
> There come now no kings nor Caesars
> Nor gold-giving lords like those gone.
>   (*EPEW* 50)

The world's glory ages and fades and one is left with nothing.

Behind "The Seafarer" is the *Odyssey* and Pound's "translation" is a precursor of his later quest poems, *Mauberley* and *The Cantos*. In "The Constant Preaching to the Mob," a 1916 essay, he clearly associates the Anglo-Saxon poem with Book XI of the *Odyssey*, the basis of Canto I (*LE* 64). In his essay, an incensed Pound, upset at the middle-class response to poetry only as entertainment, emphasizes individual suffering and courage in both the *Odyssey* and "The Seafarer," identifying the poets with their heroes. For Pound they become personae of the artist-as-Odysseus, as his later work will elaborate.

The importance of "The Seafarer" for Pound is largely in his free play of translation and use of meter, which he would try to adapt to Homer. In 1916, in fact, he told the young writer Iris Barry that he tried an adaptation of the Anglo-Saxon meter for the poem but few would likely recognize the source. But what Pound values most in the poem is its robust self-exposure, ironically unsuited to an epic, which favors impersonality. "The Seafarer" is, in fact, elegiac, not epic, although Pound, nevertheless, uses its meter in Canto I.

"The Return" is another important work in *Ripostes* because Pound experiments metrically with the strophe. Here, the Sapphic stanza has a shadow presence as a sort of musical theme:

> See, they return; ah, see the tentative
>   Movements, and the slow feet,
>   The trouble in the pace and the uncertain
> Wavering!   (*EPPT* 244)

The analogy Pound set for the poem was not music but sculpture, as he notes in *Gaudier-Brzeska*. There, he comments that the poem "is an objective reality and has a complicated sort of significance," adding that such poems "are Imagisme, and . . . they fall in with the new pictures and the new sculpture" (*GB* 85).

Several texts in *Ripostes* and other works at this time suggest a restricted Platonism as in "Paracelsus in Excelsis" or "Blandulla, tenulla, vagula," both from *Canzoni* (1911), as Pound seeks a poetry transcending time and place rather than a poetry that is dense with the particulars of history. In fact, the wish to transcend history may be stronger than Pound's desire to act in history. *The Cantos* seem governed by a conviction that the poet has to earn the right to such transcendence, but only after history is understood.

Beginning in 1912, Pound was exploring another line of poetry in an effort to break free from the mimetic. He named this new form Imagism as he presented new conventions of non-representational art. Emanating from the tea room at the British Museum when Pound slashed through H. D.'s poem "Hermes of the Ways" and signed it "H. D. Imagiste," the movement purged poetry of excessive rhetoric and overly stated imagery through the "direct treatment of the 'thing'" (*LE* 3). The process excluded inessential details in the pursuit of significant particulars. Symbolism, by contrast, dealt with association and allusion; the image is immediate and direct and "is the furthest possible remove from rhetoric" (*GB* 83). Symbolists' symbols have "a fixed value" but Imagists' images "have a variable significance." The former is like arithmetic, the latter like algebra (*GB* 84). Browning's *Sordello* is "one of the finest *masks* ever presented" but "Dante's *Paradiso* is the most wonderful *image*" (*GB* 86). Pound's "A Few Don'ts by an Imagist" and "Affirmations, As for Imagisme" outline his approach, which his anthology *Des Imagistes* (1914) confirms. In "Affirmations," for example, he explains that the "Image is more than an idea. It is a vortex or cluster of fused ideas and is endowed with energy" (*EPEW* 293).

Pound's account of how he wrote "In a Station of the Metro" crystallizes the Imagist method. The process began in 1911 when he emerged from the Metro at La Concorde in Paris and saw a series of beautiful faces. "I tried all that day to find words for what this had meant to me" but he could not – nothing to equal "that sudden emotion." That evening, almost unconsciously, he found the expression, actually splotches of color, "a word, the beginning, for me, of a language in colour" (*GB* 87). He realized that there was as much "pleasure in an arrangement of planes or in a pattern of figures, as in painting portraits of fine ladies" (*GB* 87).

The single-image poem was his escape, or rather his discovery of how to make the Imagist poem. He originally wrote a thirty-line Metro poem but destroyed it. Six months later, he fashioned a poem half that length, a year later formulated into:

> The apparition of these faces in the crowd:
> Petals, on a wet, black bough.

Such a poem, he explains, is an attempt to record "the precise instant when a thing outward and objective transforms itself, or darts into a thing inward and subjective" (*GB* 89). Pound then carefully distinguishes Imagism from Vorticism, which he developed with Wyndham Lewis and which BLAST expressed.

Vorticism "is an intensive art" seeking the most intense means of expression, Pound writes. In an advertisement for BLAST in the *Spectator*, the text claims the journal as a movement and the "Death blow to Impressionism and Futurism."[3] Using mathematical equations, Pound shows how Vorticism gains its power. The Image is not an idea but "a radiant node or cluster." It is a VORTEX "from which, and through which, and into which, ideas are constantly rushing" (*GB* 90, 92). The energetic structuring of forms might be another formulation of the Vorticist aesthetic and, while "organized fury" might slightly overstate the case, it conveys the management of form and intensity Vorticism sought. At one point, Pound carefully separates it from Futurism which he calls "a kind of accelerated impressionism" (*GB* 90). He also relates Vorticism to sculpture, especially that of Gaudier-Brzeska and Jacob Epstein, both of whom use the "relation of planes" in a new geometric fashion to define or re-define mass. The organization of forms, he repeats, is energetic and its work non-mimetic. Wyndham Lewis's *Timon*, Edward Wadsworth's "Khaki," and the work of Gaudier-Brzeska and Epstein stand as examples, although, after 1914, Vorticism lost much of its currency.

Vorticisim's energy, ironically, became its downfall. In 1922, John Cournos presented a fictional satire of the movement in his novel *Babel* where the Vorticists become the "Dynamists." He links their machine aesthetic to a mood of national unity at the outbreak of the First World War as the anti-humanist abstractions of Vorticism suddenly appear to join the dehumanized violence of war. Masculinized aggression and sexuality were linked, expressed in part by Gaudier-Brzeska's *Hieratic Head of Pound*, displayed in May 1914, one month before the first issue of BLAST – which lasted only two issues. But the war disrupted the movement and dissipated its whirlpool of energy, partly as the result of the death of Gaudier-Brzeska at the front. In *The Pisan Cantos*, however, Pound recalls the importance of the movement.

Pound remained intrigued by the Machine, seeing in its operation a metaphor of integration which managed to produce an individual product. "Machine Art," his essay of 1927–30, would develop the seemingly contradictory idea that individuality may be the product of the machine which dominates modern society. Earlier, he often used machine imagery to define the artist.

Writing in "Affirmations," for example, he distinguished between subjective and artistic man through mechanical references:

> Where the voltage is so high that it fuses the machinery, one has merely the "emotional man" not the artist. The best artist is the man whose machinery can stand the highest voltage. The better the machinery, the more precise, the stronger, the more exact will be the record of the voltage and of the various currents which have passed through it.   (*EPEW* 295)

The artist is not passive. He records but also creates.

One of the most sustained examples of Pound's focus on poetic precision is *Cathay* (1915) where he poeticized a number of Fenollosa's line-by-line translations of works by the Chinese poet Li Po. They are remarkable for their poise and concreteness. Pound worked with the notebooks of Fenollosa and other manuscripts, the notebooks containing Chinese characters for the original poems, followed by Japanese pronunciations and rough translations. Pound chose Japanese names for the Chinese poets as he worked through the material. The original edition of *Cathay* had eleven poems, including Pound's translation of the Anglo-Saxon "The Seafarer," to show the similarity of T'ang Dynasty and Anglo-Saxon views of exile. When the volume appeared as a section of *Lustra*, Pound added five more poems and dropped "The Seafarer" which appeared elsewhere in the collection.

In all the translations, detail is supreme. In "The River Song," for example, the detail of a boat as it drifts is overshadowed by the narrator's concentrated, creative eye:

> King So's terraced palace
> > is now but barren hill,
> But I draw pen on this barge
> Causing the five peaks to tremble,
> And I have joy in these words
> > like the joy of blue islands.
>
> > > (*EPEW* 61)

Further detail outlines the boredom and lack of stimulation for the Emperor's poet as he awaits:

> an order-to-write!
> I looked at the dragon pond, with its willow-coloured water
> Just reflecting the sky's tinge
> And heard the five-score nightingales aimlessly singing
>
> > (*EPEW* 61–2)

Notice that Pound numbers the nightingales.

"Song of the Bowmen of Shu" emphasizes the condition of the warriors who in a break from battle gather fern shoots. But they have "sorrowful minds" and

> . . . sorrow is strong, we are hungry and thirsty.
> Our defence is not yet made sure, no one can let his friend return.

In a line, Pound summarizes the very situation of soldiers: "there is no ease in royal affairs, we have no comfort." Even the Emperor's horses are tired; "Our mind is full of sorrow, who will know of our grief?" (*EPEW* 59, 60). In concentrated language, Pound is able to convey the anxiety of the soldiers who are now exhausted mentally and physically from battle. Pound actually sent this poem and two others to Gaudier-Brzeska at the front; he replied that the poems depict our situation "in a wonderful way" (*GB* 58), noting also that you become hardened when you become a warrior: "like the Chinese bowmen in Ezra's poem, we had rather eat fern shoots than go back now" (in *PE* 203).

"The Exile's Letter," published in *Poetry* in March 1915, was a favorite of Pound's; he reprinted it in *Cathay* and *Umbra* (1920). Pound often cited "The Exile's Letter," with "The Seafarer" and "Homage to Sextus Propertius," as his major early works. In *Cathay*, "The Exile's Letter" immediately preceded "The Seafarer" to emphasize their similarity. The exiled speaker in the poem begins by recalling a time when he and So-Kin had pleasurable times, "And we all spoke out our hearts and minds, and without regret." Then they had to separate, having only "thoughts and memories in common." Further adventures divide the two, although they occasionally re-meet:

> And what a reception:
> Red jade cups, food well set on a blue jeweled table,
> And I was drunk, and had no thought of returning.
> And you would walk out with me to the western corner of the castle,
> To the dynastic temple, with water about it clear as blue jade. . .
> And the water, a hundred feet deep, reflecting green eyebrows
>
> (*EPEW* 65–6)

Later meetings end with similar separations, however, and:

> if you ask how I regret that parting:
> It is like the flowers falling at Spring's end
> Confused, whirled in a tangle
>
> (*EPEW* 67)

Anticipating themes he would develop in the late *Cantos* – the strength of love and importance of action – Pound concludes the poem with "what is the use of talking, and there is no end of talking, / There is no end of things in the heart" (*EPEW* 67). Pound in this poem merges longing with emotion and nature, through images that are direct and clear. The Imagistic properties of the poems are evident, although Pound employs abrupt juxtapositions of images and lines, grounded in a stable lyric voice the reader can easily identify.

The essential importance of *Cathay* is what Pound did with the poetry, making the line the unit of composition. In so doing, he created the possibility of breaking the line, of disrupting it from within, as the poet and critic Donald Davie analyzed.[4] Pound's great contribution to modern prosody, according to the critic Marjorie Perloff, is "his focus on the line rather than the larger stanzaic block." "Pound's line repeatedly violates the iambic norm, "she explains, "which is to say that it goes counter to the stress pattern inherent in English."[5] No longer would English poetry run over the verse line in order to build up larger units of movement, whether it was the strophe, Miltonic verse paragraph or sustained dramatic speech. The sentence is draped over the metrical unit, the line, submerging the pentameter by "incorporating the line into the building of larger and more intricate rhythmical units" (Davie 44). Pound found something new in making the line the unit of composition. T. S. Eliot summed it up when he wrote "Pound is the inventor of Chinese poetry for our time" (*SPO* 14).

Fenollosa's work importantly confirmed Pound's Imagist aesthetic, nowhere more clearly than in his essay "The Chinese Written Character as a Medium for Poetry," Pound's most significant editorial work up to 1923. The last topic Fenollosa studied in Japan before leaving in 1900 was the Chinese writing system and he was preparing an essay on the written character of Chinese literature. Pound would edit and publish the material in 1919; it would strongly influence his own ideas of poetry. Essentially, Fenollosa believed that Chinese characters actually represent ideas (ideograms) which present concepts in visual forms. This paralleled Imagism where Pound sought a visually focused poetry. In his *ABC of Reading* (1934) Pound would write that Fenollosa's essay was "the first definite assertion of the applicability of scientific method to literary criticism" (*ABCR* 18), also stating that Fenollosa was "perhaps too far ahead of his time to be easily comprehended" (*ABCR* 19).

In contrast to the European stress on abstraction, Chinese thought, and especially its literature as Fenollosa presented it, emphasized the concrete through a language based on sight not sound. The ideogram is not "a written sign recalling a sound" but "the picture of the thing . . . it *means* the thing of the actions or situation or quality germane to the several things that it pictures" (*ABCR* 21). Defining "red" meant linking abbreviated pictures of a rose, iron rust, cherry and flamingo. In "The Chinese Written Character," Fenollosa asks if verse written in terms of "visible hieroglyphics" can be true poetry? How can the Chinese line "imply, *as form*, the very element that distinguishes poetry from prose" (*EPEW* 307)? But Fenollosa's sense of poetry matches Pound's: "all that poetic form requires is a regular and flexible sequence, as plastic as thought itself" (*EPEW* 307). Chinese notation is more than arbitrary symbols: "it is based upon a vivid shorthand picture of the operations of nature" (*EPEW* 309). Importantly, Fenollosa understands that the ideographic roots carry in them "*a verbal idea of action*" in shorthand (*EPEW* 309–10).

Fenollosa also identifies the distinguishing feature of Chinese verse, its definiteness, or what he calls its "concrete force . . . eschewing adjectives, nouns and intransitive forms wherever we can, and seeking instead strong and individual verbs" (*EPEW* 315). Chinese words, he stresses, are *not* abstract, yet he notes that "poetry differs from prose in the concrete colors of its diction . . . poetry must render what is said, not what is merely meant" (*EPEW* 319). This Chinese poetry does. Metaphor, he continues, adds to the language, however, offering other meanings, as he reiterates in his basic theme, which Pound endorses: "Art and poetry deal with the concrete of nature" and that "poetry is finer than prose because it gives us more concrete truth in the same compass of words" (*EPEW* 321). And at one point, Fenollosa sounds more like Pound than Pound: "The more concretely and vividly we express the interactions of things the better the poetry . . . poetic thought works by suggestion, crowding maximum meaning into the single phrase pregnant, charged and luminous from within" (*EPEW* 325).

The greatness of Shakespeare *and* Chinese poetry is the wealth of transitive verbs argues Fenollosa (*EPEW* 326). The pictorialness Fenollosa identifies Pound had absorbed through Imagism, now supplemented by Fenollosa's notion of "metaphoricity" or "the use of material images to suggest immaterial relations" (*EPEW* 320). Another characteristic important to Pound was etymological stability. Meanings center about the graphic symbol and don't change.

Fenollosa was modern, articulating a concept Pound would demonstrate throughout *The Cantos* but one readers had difficulty understanding: "relations are more real and more important than the things which they relate" (*EPEW* 320). This single sentence encapsulates much of what Pound realizes in the last cantos, beginning with the Pisan section. And when Fenollosa writes, "the poet can never see too much or feel too much," Pound could only agree. Being a poet out in the world was Pound's *métier* which Fenollosa upheld (*EPEW* 328). Pound also understood that Fenollosa was essentially "telling how and why a language written in this way simply HAD TO STAY POETIC" (*ABCR* 22). This not only corroborated Pound's own ideas but confirmed his own thought and the direction his poetry was taking. Earlier in 1915, he had told Harriet

Monroe that in good writing "there must be no clichés, set phrases, stereotyped journalese. The only escape from such is by precision . . . objectivity and again objectivity" (*SL* 49). Fenollosa showed him how it was done at least in one major literature.

One of the poetic strategies emerging from the use of personae Pound was to rely on was satire, a response to what he called his "beastly and cantankerous age" ("Three Cantos" I – *EPEW* 146). He favored satire because he believed it was truthful. Pound's friction with the present encouraged a satirical stance, not only in individual poems but in many passages of *The Cantos*. And as with most of Pound's ideas, he finds a historical root which, for satire, he identifies as one of three devices of poetic restoration in Provençal writing of the thirteenth-century (*LE* 103). Interestingly, he argues in "Troubadours – Their Sorts and Conditions" that only satire allows contact "with the normal life of the time" (*LE* 103). Piere Cardinal is key because, unlike Sordello or de Born, who direct their satire at people, Piere Cardinal directs it against conditions. Pound would develop this form of satire in a variety of works, most notably in *Mauberley*. Protest through satire seemed acceptable; objection through direct political action did not. For Pound, satire is subtle and not merely abusive, but it can be sharp: "satire is surgery, insertions and amputations" (*LE* 45). Especially appealing about Cardinal's satire is the match between the sound and the meaning: "there is a lash and sting in his timbre and in his movement" (*LE* 106). Satire, Pound wrote in "The Serious Artist," "reminds one that certain things are not worthwhile"(*LE* 45).

Jules Laforge and French writing of the late nineteenth century are Pound's next source of satire. In Laforge's work, he detects a social satire akin to that of the Provençals. Pound also reads Henry James as a satirist and, in his long essay on the novelist, provides in a footnote clarification of the satiric impulse and prose style: "Most good prose arises," he writes, "from an instinct of negation . . . [a] convincing analysis of something detestable . . . Poetry is the assertion of a positive . . . [while] poetic satire is only an assertion of this positive, inversely, *i.e.* as of an opposite hatred" (*LE* 324). Later in the note, he writes "Poetry = Emotional synthesis, quite as real, quite as realist as any prose (or intellectual) analysis" (*LE* 324).

Pound's own poetic satires took various forms, many reprinted in *Lustra*. "Salutation," for example, opens with "O generation of the thoroughly smug / and thoroughly uncomfortable," while "Further Instructions" begins with "Come, my songs, let us express our baser passions, / Let us express our envy of the man with a steady job and now worry about the future" (*EPPT* 265, 273). "Meditatio" and "L'Art, 1910" are similarly sharp; "The Lake Isle," edged with humor, eases the satire, while it complains of the writing life. Satire even suffuses the magisterial "Near Perigord" as the speaker berates war and its cost.

"End fact. Try fiction" the narrator of "Near Perigord" exhorts at one point – and then imagines a situation with dramatic force and yet unresolved details, satirizing the very process of creativity:

> a lean man? Bilious?
> With a red straggling beard?
> And the green cat's-eye lifts toward Montagnac
> (*EPEW* 94)

The poem satirizes itself as Arnaut Daniel and Richard Coeur de Lion question its value:

> Is it a love poem? Did he sing of war?
> Is it an intrigue to run subtly out,
> Born of a jongleur's tongue [?]
> (*EPEW* 93)

This three-part poem is one Pound's most important early efforts in consciously exploring form and its limitations, while avoiding an ending, creating only a state of longing. Bertran de Born's love, now in Tairiran's castle, is no more than "a broken bundle of mirrors . . .!" (*EPEW* 97).

"Villanelle: The Psychological Hour" is a contemporary satire almost Prufrockian in its despair:

> I had over-prepared the event,
>   that much was ominous.
> With middle ageing care
>   I had laid out just the right books.
> I had almost turned down the pages
> (*EPEW* 89)

"The Temperaments" is equally direct, as the narrator compares the quiet and supposedly sexless Florialis and the supposedly bolder Bastidides who has become the father of twins but "had to be four times cuckold" (*EPPT* 317).

In *Lustra*, Pound experiments with satires of varying lengths, some only two lines, and others more elaborate. He also telescopes time and place, anticipating what he will do frequently in *The Cantos*. Two lines from "To a Friend Writing on Cabaret Dancers" illustrate this clearly: "'Poète, writ me a poème!' / Spanish and Paris, love of the arts part of your geisha-culture!" (*EPPT* 312). Other works like the "*Moeurs Contemporaines*" sequence in *Quia Pauper Amavi* (1919) and "Alfred Venison's Poems" (1934), which opens with a parody of Tennyson in "The Charge of the Bread Brigade," show Pound's continuing satirical nature.

The address to Sordello in Canto I of "Three Cantos of a Poem of Some Length," the first part-publication of *The Cantos*, expands the satirical tone of the shorter poems in a hesitant but clear voice:

> Hang it all, there can be but the one "Sordello,"
> But say I want to, say I take your whole bag of tricks,
> Let in your quirks and tweeks, and say the thing's an art-form,
> Your "Sordello," and that the "modern world"
> Needs such a rag-bag to stuff all its thought in.   (*EPPT* 318)

Ideas and the world are too large for an ordered form, one that is unable to contain disparate experiences from many worlds. Or, as he tells Browning, "I have my background; and you had your background" (*EPPT* 320).

Pound's satire expanded as his criticism of England and the war increased, resulting in three important texts: first, a contemporary critique of society expressed in *L'Homme Moyen Sensuel* (1917); second, a lengthy dramatic monologue set in the classical world, "Homage to Sextus Propertius" (1919); and third, his remarkable long satire, *Hugh Selwyn Mauberley* (1920). All three emphasize Pound's restlessness and disillusionment with his time, which *The Cantos* attempt to reconcile, their own structural restlessness an embodiment of his cultural unease and search – from the West to the East, from Malatesta to Confucius – for answers.

A cause of Pound's anger transmuted into satire was the war which coincided with the effort by the "men of 1914" – Wyndham Lewis's phrase for Eliot, Pound and himself – radically to modernize the visual, resulting in Vorticism, the expression of dynamic content. When England declared war on Germany on 8 August 1914, it signaled a change in European culture which would likely never be as homogeneous or productive again. Pound's first response was a set of poems in *Poetry* of March 1915: "The Coming of War: Actæon," "Provincia Deserta" and "Exile's Letter." "Provincia Deserta" (deserted province) suggests the loss Pound experienced not only with the past but in the present. Drawn from his 1912 walking tour of southern France, it discusses sites and traditions associated with Provençal that he knows has disappeared:

> That age is gone;
> Pieire de Maensac is gone.
> I have walked over these roads;
> I have thought of them living
>
>   (*EPEW* 88)

He is preparing for his own departure from England.

The three satires Pound wrote between 1917 and 1920 mark most clearly how the war had riven through culture to shatter a society and his outlook. In two of these works, one set in the classical world, the other in the contemporary, satire offers not only a critique of culture but a view of the direction his longer, still-incomplete work, *The Cantos*, would take.

L'Homme Moyen Sensuel first appeared in the *Little Review* of September 1917, the title, ("The Average Sensual Man") originating with Matthew Arnold in his essay "George Sand." The poem has further nineteenth-century roots, notably in Byronic satire which Pound imitates through nearly 200 lines of rhymed couplets. Composed in April 1915, he sent it first to *Smart Set* as a likely place for its appearance. His accompanying note told the editors to "boom it as THE SATIRE, 'best since Byron' . . . not such an awful lie, if one considers that nobody has written satire, in the best English iambic tradition, since God knows when" (*SCh* 285). *Smart Set* turned it down saying much of the meter was labored, the couplets strained.

The pointed social criticism and invective narrates the education of Radway, a young American who somewhat parallels Pound's own early experiences in America before he left for Europe. Radway doesn't leave, however, and becomes enmeshed in American popular culture. Yet the narrator indicts the mediocrity of American life and its cultural custodians, whether editors, publishers or fellow writers: "For minds so wholly founded upon quotations / Are not the best of pulse for infant nations" (*EPEW* 99). Like Dryden or Pope who railed against dullness, Pound laments the condition of Radway who does not learn from the American writers who matter: Poe, Whitman, Whistler and James, who all gained recognition in Europe.

In his effort to satirize, Pound's language gets ahead of him ("Despite it all . . . febrile concupiscence / Whose blubbering yowls you take for passion's essence"), although he tries to control his story: "I will hang simple facts / Upon a tale, to combat other tracts" but "Think, / Could Freud or Jung unfathom such a sink?" (*EPEW* 100). Pound's enthusiasm for satire and Byronic drive, however, overtake him as he describes Radway's demise into the middle-brow culture of the country. Only the press or the magazines are his substance: "They held the very marrow of the ideals / That fed his spirit; were his mental meals" (*EPEW* 101). The desire to satirize encapsulates the story of Radway's love life, parodying Shelley at one point: "I burn, I freeze, I sweat, said the fair Greek, / I speak in contradictions, so to speak" (*EPEW* 102). But an undercurrent of social issues such as sweat-shop employment, restrictive morality and censorship appear in the latter part of the poem as he criticizes the treatment of men only as social functions (*EPEW* 103). Radway, examining New York, is self-satisfied and dismissive of Prague, Vienna or Moscow. Radway becomes a recessive observer of Broadway and social life – a Prufrock of the metropolis whom Pound treats derisively: "Radway was a patriot whose venality / Was purer in its love of one locality" – at the expense of connecting culturally to the world, and becomes a professional moralist, finding his spiritual and economic life satisfied through religion (*EPEW* 104).

Pound's description is almost a self-indictment of what *he* might have become if he had stayed in America and although the poem lacks the sophistication or complication of either "Propertius" or *Mauberley*, its satirical quality indicates a poetic move Pound thought might provide a path for his later work. The importance of satire in his next two works, plus *The Cantos*, proves its importance to his poetic program.

In "Homage to Sextus Propertius" – Pound's free translation and reassembly of the Latin elegies of the poet Sextus Propertius, of which only four books survive – Pound selects and arranges the poems to create a complex and highly unorthodox portrait of Propertius, the first-century Roman poet. He finished the work in 1917, although it did not appear until 1919. The themes reflect those in much First World War verse: love, war, death and poetry. Disillusionment with war expressed through Propertius' persona contains Pound's protest, which he confirmed in a letter, underscoring his frustration at facing "the infinite and ineffable imbecility of the British Empire" as Propertius faced the "imbecility of the Roman Empire" (*SL* 231). Rather than celebrate war, Propertius will celebrate love.

"Propertius" is the first of Pound's major sequence poems. In uncovering and emphasizing the irony of Propertius in the poem, Pound frees himself from Victorian obfuscation and sentimentalizing. But when four sections of the poem appeared in *Poetry* in March 1919, it aroused the anger of the classicist W. G. Hale who attacked its numerous errors, declaring Pound ignorant of Latin. Pound answered that he had not done a translation of Propertius but attempted to restore vitality to the poet's work (*SL* 149, 229–30). The translation, he maintained, was creative, and closer to an adaptation. He adjusted the original to contemporary language rather than imitated the original through a literal translation. In his introduction to Ezra Pound, *Selected Poems* (1928), T. S. Eliot called it "a paraphrase, or still more truly . . . a *persona*" (*SPO* 19).

What made Propertius central to Pound's reading and study of poetry was the Roman poet's irony. In the earlier poet's work, Pound first identified *logopoeia*, which he defined as "the dance of the intellect among words" (*LE* 25). This attitude does not translate, although it might be captured by paraphrase. Tone and color and the state of mind of the poet, not exact expressions, are more fundamental (*SL* 231). In the poem, Pound also argues that the Victorians misread Propertius, emphasizing his sentimentality not irony. In the text, he criticizes such misreadings. Not Walter Pater but Jules Laforge, the French satirical poet, is the proper model.

"Propertius" becomes a mask for Pound, the last of the major single personae in his work. His rearrangement of the elegies, in itself a modernist gesture, creates a portrait that both interprets the historical original and reflects the preoccupations of the modern translator. The poem is the bridge between Pound's Imagist program, the influence of Fenollosa and his later works. Like *Cathay*, the poem is a free translation of ancient lyrics relying on the convention of a single, unifying speaker. It not only summarizes Pound's absorption with the classics, which marks his earliest poetic and prose efforts, but is an elegy to the Edwardian–Georgian reading public. Before the First World War, Pound took them for granted and adjusted his writing to meet their requirements. That readership would be a casualty of the war, however, with its replacement unclear. In his next and most important early poem, *Mauberley*, he details the destruction of this audience at the same time as attempting to reformulate it.

Hugh Selwyn Mauberley refined Pound's sense of sequence and structure, anticipating the form of *The Cantos*. It also encapsulates Pound's growing disenchantment with England, partly because little he wrote at this time met with praise. To Williams in September 1920 he complained that "there is no longer any intellectual *life* in England save what centres in this eight by ten pentagonal room" (*SL* 158–9). After twelve years, Pound was no longer finding England congenial to the arts. The fragmented narrative yet direct voice of *Mauberley* may be a metaphor for what is essentially an embittered social vision in which Pound condenses imagery and allusions but this time without a central speaker. But he makes it especially clear that he is "no more Mauberley than Eliot is Prufrock . . . Mauberley is a mere surface. Again a study in form, an attempt to condense the James novel. Meliora speramus" (*SL* 180).

Mauberley essentially tells the story of the conventional poet Mauberley's unhappiness with London and its culture in response to the horror of the First World War. It also alludes to influences like Henry James and Théophile Gautier. In James, Pound admired the presentation of atmosphere and impressions; in Gautier, a hardness in the verse, which he celebrated as poetry that was "austere, direct, free from emotional slither" (*LE* 12). "Medallion," the final poem in the *Mauberley* sequence, possibly by Mauberley himself, displays the hardness Pound admired in Gautier's *Emaux et Camées* ("Enamels and Cameos") of 1852.

Eighteen poems in two parts make up *Mauberley*, the first part running from "Ode" to "Envoi (1919)." The second begins with the title "Mauberley (1920)" – the combination of the title and date an unusual conflation of name and time. It ends with "Medallion" and the image of a glazed, oval face "Beneath half-watt rays" where the eyes "turn topaz" (*EPEW* 142). On the title page of

Personae (1926), Pound included a footnote to the poem since deleted: "The sequence is so distinctly a farewell to London that the reader who chooses to regard this as an exclusive American edition may as well omit it and turn at once to [*Homage to Sextus*] *Propertius.*" He omitted the Latin epigraph from the Roman poet Nemesianus, "the heart calls us into the shade," and the subtitle "Life and Contacts" in *Selected Poems* (1949) but reintroduced them in a revised version appearing in 1958, although the subtitle is reversed to read "Contacts and Life," which Pound told his publisher, James Laughlin, was "the actual order of the subject matter."[6]

Early readers of the poem understandably had difficulty distinguishing between Pound as poet, as narrator, and as the persona of Mauberley. Pound insisted they were all different but readers were less confident. And when he wrote that the poem was merely surface and an effort to condense a novel by Henry James, readers were equally perplexed, largely because, unlike a James novel, it possessed no coherent narrative tone nor linear text. Rather, the narrative focused on nuances, personal impressions and inconsistent tone, which Pound took to be Jamesian attributes (*SL* 180). Another problem was structure: were the sections linked or just arbitrarily joined? The answers can partially be found in Pound's French sources. The rhythms of Gautier and Bion, poets he had recently read for his essay "A Study in French Poets" (1918), are the models for the work, in which the title figure, Mauberley, appears only in the latter half. Mauberley, in contrast to Pound, is "a mask of the contemporary aesthete to show what the minor artist could expect from the England of the day."[7] The focus of the poem is the poet's place in society.

Beginning with the ironic "Ode" to an imagined "E. P.," a projection of Pound himself, the poet emphasizes dislocation in his effort to "resuscitate the dead art / Of poetry" whose true inspiration was Flaubert (*EPEW* 127). This is something of a mock obituary – the title of the section, translated from the French, is "Ode for the Selection of his Tomb." The poet, finding disillusionment with classical models like Homer (the source of the Greek in the passage), then suddenly shifts to his own age, exposing how commercialization and money prevent the artist from realizing his art in society. "He fished by obstinate isles" carries over the nautical imagery of Homer into the artistically difficult modern times to which he does not adjust (*EPEW* 127). Aesthetic concerns have disappeared.

Democracy has also corrupted itself (II, III). Sections IV and V are the climax of Pound's denunciation, as the young die for a diseased tradition, although such a theme was evident earlier in "Propertius": "Now if ever it is time to cleanse Helicon" he writes at the start of the fifth section of "Propertius," continuing by remarking that "the primitive ages sang Venus, / the last sings of a tumult" (*EPEW* 113). In *Mauberley*, however, the language is more direct, the corruption endemic: "The age demanded an image / Of its accelerated grimace." The war-weary return to "a lie, / home to many deceits, / home to old lies and new infamy." Too many died, he laments, "for an old bitch gone in the teeth, / For a botched civilization" (*EPEW* 128, 130).

The sources of this decay are, for the poet, clear: the overpowering of Pre-Raphaelite aesthetics by the official morality of Gladstone and Ruskin, an attitude that neutralized creativity and the imagination. "E. P." himself, the persona of Pound, announced on the title page and parallel to Pound in his early London years, has also been compromised by his times because he failed to modernize. His style has been trapped by old-fashioned ideals of beauty that have rigidified his language. The age has changed but not the literature. The "Yeux Glauques" section ("Glaucous Eyes," a phrase used by Gautier to evoke the dull, gray-green gaze common in Pre-Raphaelite portraits of women) provides a condensed portrait of the Pre-Raphaelite period and its aftermath, moving rapidly from Ruskin and Rossetti to the Rhymers Club of the 1890s, Max Beerbohm ("Brennbaum"), Arnold Bennett ("Mr. Nixon") and Ford Madox Ford. But again, Pound does it through the voice of another, in this case Mr. Verog, who represents the minor poet and critic Victor Plarr, author of *In the Dorian Mood* (1896). Verog speaks, in the "Siena mi fe; Disfecemi Maremma" section, Dante's phrase which means: "Siena made me; Maremma undid me" (*Purgatorio* V). London is the modern Maremma undoing the Rhymers, a process which Plarr recounts.

In Sections XI and XII, Pound shifts from the artists to the audience, satirizing various representatives of popular taste, showing, for example, an educated woman who inherits sterile traditions she does not understand (XI). In XII Pound provides a self-examination and finds he does not belong in the fashionable circles of literary London: "Knowing my coat has never been / Of precisely the fashion," as he awaits Lady Valentine, an ironic presentation of aristocratic patronage (*EPEW* 134). He bows out with a love lyric, again emphasizing title and date. "Envoi (1919)," however, contradicts the surface judgments of the critics in the opening "Ode" to the poem, showing that "E. P.," who had been "out of key with his time," can recover the sublime (*EPEW* 127).

"Mauberley 1920" begins the second part of the poem, replacing the active Pound with the aesthete, tracing the effect of cultural change on the poet, Mauberley, who begins as an Imagist but turns to a kind of indulgent impressionism. Pound models the quatrains and cameo technique of the poet on the hard surface technique of Gautier's *Emaux et Camées*. "Firmness, / not the full smile" he writes in Section I (*EPEW* 137). Here, Pound's "impersonality" reigns as he traces the career of Mauberley, not his own. Mauberley's goal is to incorporate the values of clear presentation in his work, parallel to the distinct profiles on classical medallions. The presentational style of Flaubert is his desired method but his art is not vigorous. Mauberley drifts in bewilderment, uncertain psychologically, and poetically embodied in the broken speech patterns of Section II.

Mauberley, the poet, drifts into a refined subjectivity and stops writing entirely:

> The glow of porcelain
> Brought no reforming sense
> To his perception
> Of the social inconsequence.

He prefers "Mildness, amid the neo-Nietzschean clatter" and, soon, "unexpected palms" destroy the artist's urge (*EPEW* 139, 140). Mauberley abandons the Odyssean quest; his epitaph laconically reads:

> I was
> And I no more exist;
> Here drifted
> An hedonist
>   (*EPEW* 141)

The decline of this modern Elpenor parallels the fallen crewman of Odysseus who asks the hero to set up his oar and inscribe on his tomb an epitaph which reads "A man of no fortune, with a name to come." "Medallion," at the end, is a characteristic product of Mauberley's "porcelain reverie," a static representation of beauty based on allusion and simile. The poem is only a visual record of a porcelain reality where the woman's eyes become gems, petrified and inert.

But *Mauberley* is more than a surface of fractured narratives. The façade is complex, its base appearing simple, a disparity that disconcerts at first or even second reading. This occurs partly because images imply entire arguments. Pound fits his substance with a surface at times at odds with his meaning. His emphasis on craft has shifted an emphasis from substance, but it exists in the poem which flows into the medium itself rather than into plot, myth or poetic convention. He has succeeded in making the narrative, in all its guises, new. Dissociation describes the change, one that exists not only structurally between the first and second parts of the poem but also between Pound, as the poet of passion for whom emotion is intellectual instigation, and Mauberley, the poet of beauty for whom relationships become frozen (Espey 82). The active instigator versus the passive aesthete might be one configuration of the difference as Pound was himself, at the end of 1918, preparing to replace poetry with politics. In *Mauberley*, Pound rejects the mask of what he feared he might become if he remained in England. The next year he left for Paris.

Mauberley, however, also had a positive aspect. It provided a way for Pound to break the impasse of *The Cantos*. By 1919, he had written seven – but not solved the formal problems presented by "Three Cantos" (1917) – of which six would eventually be rewritten and rearranged. *Mauberley*, however, showed him ways in which to use the mythical method he was reading in Joyce's *Ulysses*, which he had started in 1917. In May 1922, "Canto VIII" (which would later become Canto II) appeared in the *Dial*, the same month as his review of *Ulysses*, and Pound was underway again, with an intensive period of composition lasting the next three years. In July 1923, he published the "Malatesta Cantos" and, shortly after, revised the opening of the poem, in which he took the Nekuia episode from the end of Canto III and moved it to Canto I. The scaffold of his long work had changed, partly the result of *Mauberley* and the realization that the way to make the big poem work might be to find a series of historical heroes. Or, as he wrote in a letter of 1 November 1924 to his father, he was "trying to find some bhlooming historic character who can be used as illustration of intelligent constructivity" (in Witemeyer 177).

Satire continued in *The Cantos* in many guises. Indeed, he explained to one writer that the *Iliad* and the *Odyssey* both contain satire and that "I cannot believe that satire is in itself alien to epos" (*SL* 239). Numerous passages in *The Cantos* demonstrate this. It appears in Canto XXVII, for example, when the Graces confront a comrade, a plodding political man unable, it seems, to respond to the antique beauties that hover about him. Canto XXIX satirizes Neo-Platonism through the character of the short-sighted Juventus. With Pound's project approaching a Dadaist model, as some believe, because it structures itself on permutations, the entire work assumes a satirical character. Canto XXXVIII, for example, describes Marconi kneeling before the Pope because it seems the Pope has lost his power of spiritual transmission. Marconi, inventor of the radio, seems to have inherited it via radio waves which substitute for beams of divine guidance (XXXVIII/187).

Part of the purpose of Pound's satire was to recapture "the radiant world where one thought cuts through another with clean edge" and renew "a world of moving energies" (*LE* 154). Even his reading of Joyce is as a satirist, noting in a May 1922 review of *Ulysses* the presence of satire throughout, citing in particular the "sentimento-rhetorical journalism" Joyce presents at the end of

"Cyclops." Pound calls it "perhaps the most savage bit of satire we have had since Swift suggested a cure for famine in Ireland" (*EPEW* 338–9).

The Cantos

"There is no mystery about the Cantos, they are the tale of the tribe," Pound wrote in 1938 after fifty-one cantos had been published (*GK* 194). Others disagreed, however, finding the work erratic, difficult and certainly complex. Pound himself anticipated these reactions to the poem when in September 1915 he wrote to a correspondent that he was "at work on a cryselephantine poem of immeasurable length which will occupy me for the next four decades unless it becomes a bore" (in *ST* 184). The documentary nature of the poem – Pound quoting, borrowing, referring to and citing other texts, from the letters of Malatesta to those of John Adams and Confucius – made allusions, imagery and even structure difficult to follow. As Basil Bunting remarked, "the Cantos refer, but do not present" (in *SCh* 898). Even Pound did not know what he was undertaking, writing to Joyce in 1917 that "I have begun an endless poem, of no known category . . . all about everything" (*P/J* 102).

The origin of Pound's style was oral, and his new norm, speech. The very title of the sequential poem evokes music, a canto being that part of a musical score having the melody or air. It originates with the Latin *cantus*, or "song." Writing in the long poem, however, becomes layered, largely "quotation, quotation newly energized, as a cyclotron augments the energies of common particles circulating," as Hugh Kenner noted (*PE* 126).

From the start, Pound had an idea of what he wanted to do, modeled initially on Dante's *Divine Comedy* and Homer's *Odyssey*. It was a grand poem, but one that was elastic in form, capable of including more than a single hero on a journey to Paradise or return home. He expressed his conception of the poem when he stated that "an epic is a poem including history," combined with it being "a tale of the tribe "(*ABCR* 46; *GK* 194). Combining history with cultural identity fashioned a work that drew from America as much as from Europe, the two linked by parallel themes of individuality, rebellion and the attempt to establish a culture. Between the old and new worlds stood China, the focus of Cantos LII–LXI, while climaxing the work is the self, expressed through memory when Pound wrote, without reference books, manuscripts or histories, *The Pisan Cantos*. This portion (Cantos LXXIV–LXXXIV) is essentially a memory poem in which he uses the present and its deprivations at the Disciplinary Training Center as an entry to the past, so that memory and the moment blend. The overall result is a work with peaks and valleys, clarity and confusion, a monumental example of how the long poem can be written in the twentieth century: not with the linear development of the *Divine Comedy* but with digression, diversion and at times disorder – yet with an emotional intensity and engagement with history few works can match.

To his father, from Rapallo, Pound offered an early summary of *The Cantos*, as he struggled with its structure, in the odd remark that the shape would be "rather like, or unlike subject and response and counter subject in fugue:

> A. A. Live man goes down into world of Dead
> C. B. The "repeat in history"
> B. C. The "magic moment" or moment of metamorphosis, bust thru
>   from quotidien into "divine or permanent world." Gods, etc.

(SL 210)

To a reader some years later, he outlined the way to read the work: "skip anything you don't understand and go on till you pick it up again. All tosh about *foreign languages* making it difficult." Some of the Greek might be challenging, he admits, but if he can "drive the reader to learning at least that much Greek, she or he will indubitably be filled with a durable gratitude" (*SL* 250–1).

Unsure himself as to how the entire work would evolve, Pound labeled his volumes, when they began to appear in book form, "drafts": *A Draft of XVI. Cantos* (1925), *A Draft of the Cantos 17–27* (1928) and then *A Draft of XXX Cantos* (1930), all to suggest the unfinished state of the work, allowing him to revise or restructure – which he did with the earliest published sections. After "Three Cantos" appeared in *Poetry* in 1917, he took the material from Canto III and made it Canto I in 1925, now providing the opening that has become standard for the poem: "And then went down to the ship, / Set keel to breakers, forth on the godly sea" (I/3). The abbreviated but powerful language originally initiated the action of Book XI of *The Odyssey* and the descent of Odysseus to the underworld, Pound now joining a tradition of chthonic poets including Virgil. Unusual about this opening canto, however, is that Pound is beginning with a translation of a translation.

Pound's source text is not Homer but Andreas Divus's sixteenth-century Latin translation which he found in Paris. Yet the *in medias res* opening thrusts the reader into the action: the curious "And then" opening. This is truly "the tale of the tribe," a mythic opening – the journey to the underworld – repeated in countless literatures, which Pound makes new by the energy, vigor and immediacy of the action. We are briskly underway, moving through a polyphonic intellectual autobiography. It simultaneously manifests a history of literature and culture at the same time that it questions, tests and revises the categories we establish to conceive them. Recurrence, often through myth, determines its movement, supported by history and the self. Flux, openness and a kind of poetry of quotation substitute for the regulated, closed verse of either statement or self-consciousness.

Not surprisingly, the poem contains an encyclopedic range of allusions and references that include the classical world of Greece, the European Renaissance of Italy, the T'sung dynasty of China, the American War of Independence, and Europe before and during the Second World War. Languages include Greek, Latin, French, Chinese, German, Provençal and English. Even when the language and references become jumbled, the surface gives a clue, Pound claimed. Of Canto XX, dealing with Niccolo d'Este's reaction to the execution of Parisina and Ugo, he says it should be taken "as a sort of bounding surface from which one gives the main subject of the Canto, the *lotophagoi*: lotus eaters" (*SL* 210).

Dates and documents are another feature. Pound interlaces his poem with numerous dates of events, texts, battles and travels. They stand as bald expressions of history at the same time as seeming to be questioned: Mozart signs a letter August 1777 (XXVI/128), Bucentoro sings in:

> 1908, 1909, 1910, and there was
> An old washerwoman beating her washboard,
> that would be 1920   (XXVII/129–30)

Canto XLVI ends with the date 1527, a report of "19 years on this case." "FIVE million youths without jobs" refers to the US Depression, followed by the figures "FOUR million adult illiterates / 15 million 'vocational misfits'" and "NINE million persons injured in industrial accidents" (XLVI/234–5). All this is in the "3rd year of the reign of F. Roosevelt" and then the year "a.d. 1935" (XLVI/235). Mathematics competes with language as an anchor for the poem. Numbers mark the past ("that was Padre José Elizondo / in 1906 and in 1917" [LXXXI/537]), identify the present ("8th October: / Si tuit li dolh elh plor" [LXXXIV/ 557]) and suggest a future. Numbers are a shorthand for history – see LXXXVI/584 – and regulate the poem, as do the various musical figures and notes that appear in the text (LXXV/470–1).

Documents are also omnipresent and integrated with the text, prose often mingling with poetry. In Canto IX, dates and documents run together as Pound excerpts letters from Lunarda da Palla (20 December 1454) and Malatesta (*this the 22nd day of December / anno domini 1454*) (IX/39). In Canto X documents seem to control the text with a long Latin excerpt from "*Yriarte, p 288*" on Malatesta forming a portion of the canto (X/44). Later in the poem, various dates again work to identify or particularize moments, something of an irony given the critical view of Pound's ahistorical representation of themes.

In Canto XLVI, for example, when discussing the court case against usury, we read

> Seventeen years on the case; here
> Gents, is/are the confession.
>   "Can we take this into court?
>   "Will any jury convict on this evidence?
>   1694 anno domini, on through the ages of usury
>   (XLVI/233)

In the same Canto, dates and art unite:

> 1527. Thereafter art thickened. Thereafter design went to hell,
> Thereafter barocco, thereafter stone-cutting desisted.
> "Hic nefas" (narrator) "commune sepulchrum"
>   (XLVI/234)

Translated, the last line reads "here is infamy . . . the common sepulcher." Before 1931, Pound wrote "certainly the metamorphosis into carnal tissue becomes frequent and general somewhere about 1527. The people are corpus, corpuscular" and the body no longer "radiates, light no longer moves from the eye" (*LE* 153).

Numbers in so many ways act as markers for Pound, suggesting a kind of scientific, or at least objective, means to measure change. Years mark or measure moments of history and he constantly cites them, whether in relation to America, Europe or Asia (XLVI/235). Money detailed in figures is also another form of numerical expression used by Pound (LXXIV/460) who favored dating his letters from Italy using the Fascist calendar which employed Roman rather than Arabic numerals. He duplicated this in the numbering system of *The Cantos*, all Roman.

Equally objective in form is Pound's use of parataxis as he arranges, but does not integrate, a "phalanx of particulars" (LXXIV/461). A method of presenting materials side by side without commenting on their relation to one another, parataxis questions or denies relations of similarity and identity. It is up to the reader to fashion connections. For Pound, this is the extension of his "two-image" juxtapositions of Vorticist thought through the large-scale collage form of *The Cantos* and even portions of the *ABC of Reading*. The technique invites consideration of both similarity and difference. Pound wants his readers to connect and disconnect. However, the essential feature of parataxis is to avoid assertions about the relations between its elements. It preserves differences while on the surface it suggests similarities. Or, as Pound stated in the first part of his early series "I Gather the Limbs of Osiris," "We advance by discriminations, by discerning that things hitherto deemed identical or similar are dissimilar; that things hitherto deemed dissimilar, mutually foreign, antag-onistic, are similar and harmonic" (*SP* 25). The task of the reader of *The Cantos* is to be co-creator of the text and co-worker in the process of culture-making.

However, although the basic structure of *The Cantos* is paratactic, it also exhibits seriality. Known in music as serialism, this formal method emphasizes a sequence which underlies surface disparity. In poetry, it is a way of structur-ing long, sectional yet lyric poems as a *series* of meditative leaps, paratactic in relation, presenting serious issues without narration but by a kind of connected "tacking" from point to point. Seriality was a possible solution to the question of modernist form, resolving binary constructions of lyric meditation vs. ency-clopedic collage. The resulting "meditative collage" describes Poundian works like *Mauberley*, as well as *The Cantos*. Fragment and meditation mix, just as do the lyric and collage.

Serialism in music, associated with Arnold Schoenberg's twelve-tone scale and later with Webern, Berg and Stravinsky, developed at about the same time Pound was writing *The Cantos*: Schoenberg's *Piano Suite, Op. 25* is dated 1924; Webern's *String Quartet, Op. 28*, 1938. Both are considered classic examples of serial music, the ordering of pitch, dynamics, rhythm and instrumentation in a row or series in which each gradation is assigned a numerical value within the series. The use of mathematical concepts to control musical parameters appealed to many and is broadly similar to Pound's attempt to objectify poetry through Imagism and numbers. His almost algebraic explanations of poetic form (see "Vorticism," *EPEW* 287–9; *ABC of Reading*) approach the method, although without the intensity of the serial composers. Yeats sensed this in "A Packet for Ezra Pound" when he outlined the possible structure of *The Cantos* and wrote that "the mathematical structure, when taken up into imagination, is more than mathematical" (*AV* 5).

Serialism is a response to the demise of tonal music which resolved around a home note, a tonic, and relieved musical and structural tension. At first such notes seemed dissonant and harsh to listeners, and apparently formless. The listener is aware only of unrepeated and unpredictable musical events which dissolve in and out of each other in an apparently random fashion. The response is similar to first readings of, and reactions to, Pound's work. But, gradually, it was understood that a harmonic succession of notes resulting from a controlled juxtaposition of row forms provided serial music with its coherence. It was understood that *The Cantos* had a shape.

Not surprisingly, structure is perhaps the biggest challenge to readers of *The Cantos* and one may legitimately ask: does *The Cantos* have a form? The text is not ordered with a structured plot or series of developing characters as in epics of previous eras, although Pound reminds us that "there's a corking plot to the *Iliad*, but it is not told us in the poem" (*LE* 394). Our modern situation is one of misdirection and yet discovery, Pound believes, reflected in the instability of the entire *Cantos* project. He summarizes the situation when he writes in "Cavalcanti" that the world has lost its clarity (*LE* 154). We should not despair but respond as best we can with fragments, broken phrases, and the voice of others, as well as our own. Or as Yeats said of *The Cantos* in 1928, "there will be no plot, no chronicle of events, no logic of discourse, but two themes, the Descent into Hades . . . a Metamorphosis from Ovid, and mixed with these, mediaeval or modern historical characters" (*AV* 3–5).

Essentially, however, the structure or outline of *The Cantos*, corresponding to their publication in book form, takes this shape: Cantos I–XVI (*A Draft of XVI Cantos*, 1925) open with mythical and legendary materials including Odysseus' descent to Hades, and troubadour and Italian parallels to Ovid. Modern life, by contrast, is shown to be empty. Providing a degree of coherence to the section are the Malatesta Cantos, Cantos VIII–XI. They focus on the struggle of this fifteenth-century ruler of Rimini to bring culture to the city, notably through the construction of the Tempio Malatestiano, actually the Church of San Francesco designed by Leon Batista Alberti and built as a monument to Malatesta and his mistress, Isotta, later his third wife. Pound was fascinated by his life and fusion of Renaissance art and power. Pound visited the church in May 1922. The impact of the story of Malatesta on Pound was profound, creating the first sustained section of *The Cantos*, recalled in Chapter 24 of *Guide to Kulchur* (159–60)

Malatesta's Tempio acts as kind of symbol of the poem in its attempt to mix paganism and the Church, an architectural achievement and failure (while Isotta's tomb was built, the building remained unfinished). It blended ecclesiastical architecture and Roman triumphal art. By contrast, the interior sculptural decorations have Greek connotations: neo-Platonic and Pythagorean allusions. The building curiously upheld two conflicting ideologies, later reaffirmed when it was discovered that Malatesta interred there the ashes of a neo-Platonist philosopher, Plethon, who helped to revive Greek learning. Malatesta, himself, was known to be cultured and treacherous, as a nineteenth-century biography of him, studied by Pound, made clear. Pound adopted the Homeric epithet of "POLUMETIS" or "many minded" for him in the poem (IX/36).

The balance of the first sixteen Cantos criticize modern monopolies, idealize the order associated with Confucianism, and balance an escape to the Elysian fields (the opening of XVI) with the brutality of the First World War (close of XVI). Pound also began to insert historical figures and foreign speech which gave the verse a jagged linguistic quality. Large sections of XVI, for example, narrate the experiences of many in the war, from Richard Aldington to Gaudier-Brzeska, T. E. Hulme, Wyndham Lewis and Hemingway (XVI/71–2), while other pages are in French (XVI/72–4). Paradise, he suggests, is never complete, nor permanent. The Russian Revolution, with reference to Trotsky, Lenin and its brutal beginning, ends Canto XVI.

A Draft of the Cantos 17–27 appeared in 1928 and it, again, operates by juxtaposition, highlighting a return to Venice, modern profiteers and Renaissance life (XVII). The world is at first placid if not pastoral:

> So that the vines burst from my fingers
> And the bees weighted with pollen
> Move heavily in the vine-shoots.
>
> (XVII/76)

The "Cave of Nerea" brings comfort and nature is beauty. But, by XVIII, the world becomes one of greed and power, with a corresponding shift in diction:

> And the first thing Dave lit on when they got there
> Was a buzz-saw,
> And he put it through an ebony log: whhsssh, t ttt,
> Two days' work in three minutes.
>
> War, one war after another,
> Men start 'em who couldn't put up a good hen-roost.
>
> Also sabotage . . .   (XVIII/83)

Cantos XXIV–XXVII begin by recounting more of the life of Niccolo d'Este, his travels through the Mediterranean and benevolence as a ruler, although the main theme of these cantos is Venice – not the glittery, but the muddy, Venice, sinking into the Adriatic. The remainder of these cantos to XXVII provides a series of substitute paradises, although Pound said in Canto XX, "various things keep cropping up in the poem." The very core of its structure is, in fact, contingent, irregular and exciting (*SL* 210). Of Canto XX he remarked on its "subject-rhyme," a term implying that Pound has altered rhyme from a technique to a theme: history itself seems to express a sort of stanza form. Economics also begins to appear through the exploiters of labor and the power of merchants. Their patron is Kubla Khan, not the builder of Xanadu as in Coleridge, but the debaser of currency.

Purgatory, not Paradise, begins to shadow the work. Pound was now working toward a chronological asymmetry, a kind of recursive use of time, although it had to evolve. *A Draft of XVI Cantos*, for example, still displays a distinct chronological structure – but time actually becomes scrambled, one of the challenges in understanding the poem. Dada and its re-ordering of time and structure is an influence with even satire more directly entering the Cantos, as in XXVII as the Graces confront tovarisch, a comrade incapable of responding to either beauty or direction: "'Can you tell the down from the up?'" (XXVII/132).

Cantos XXVIII–XLI, in *A Draft of XXX Cantos* (1930), and then *Eleven New Cantos* (1934), right the drift of *The Cantos* toward farce. The three new Cantos that complete the thirty (XXVIII–XXX) return to myth with a near-burlesque of neo-Platonism as a youthful Juventus glimpses a metaphysical universe (XXIX/142–3), although still with satire as he remarks that "the wail of the phonograph has penetrated their marrow" (XXIX/143). Again, everyday existence intercuts the mythical with the Darwinian. As the narrator remarks, "The young seek comprehension; / The middleaged to fulfill their desire" (XXIX/144). The Canto ends with a lyrical passage condensing image and nature, evocative of *Cathay*:

> The cut cool of the air,
> Blossom cut on the wind, by Helios
> Lord of the Light's edge, and April
> Blown round the feet of the God . . .
> (XXIX/145–6)

Eleven New Cantos introduces Thomas Jefferson (although he was mentioned in Canto XXI). Pound later titled these so-called "Jefferson Cantos" as "Jefferson – Nuevo Mundo," to emphasize the originator of the Declaration of Independence who was also the third president of the United States. No longer is flux and movement the central theme. A new sense of direction and decidability takes over: from the wilderness, a country, from disorganization, order. The eleven cantos draw extensively from the letters of Jefferson at two different phases of his career: (1) the revolutionary period and immediately after, when Jefferson was ambassador to Paris; and then (2) when he was retired. Out of quotation and fragment, Pound draws a vivid portrait of an instrumental figure for the poem joining Confucius, John Adams and Mussolini.

In these cantos, Pound introduces the New World and the American Founding Fathers to contrast with the darkness and decay of the Old World in Europe. His later essay "The Jefferson–Adams Letters as a Shrine and a Monument" (1937–8) restates his analysis of America's revolutionary importance and what he calls "a still workable dynamo left us from the real period," Jefferson's correspondence (*SP* 117). Reductively, he emphasizes that "CIVILISATION WAS in America" (*SP* 117). A study of Jefferson's correspondence with Adams is a foundation for understanding not only American history but literature, Pound asserts. Their writings also exhibit "excellent prose" largely because they possess the "integrity of the word" (*SP* 118). His essay goes on to analyze the nature of

American culture and what steps need to be taken to fulfill its promise, praising, among other things, the correspondents' knowledge of Latin (*SP* 123).

Jefferson's letters define national culture better than anything else Pound argues, although in his characteristic style, he sets up Jefferson with certain "axes of reference" (*SP* 119). This Poundian method places Jefferson in the context of Henry Adams, John Quincy Adams and European movements ("As Americans we are neither Teutonic nor in any strict sense Mediterranean, though we should be fools to neglect either element of private nutrition" [*SP* 118]). Developing ideas of a "Mediterranean paideuma," the essay stands as an important statement of Poundian cultural analysis and method (*SP* 120).

In *Jefferson and/or Mussolini* (1935), Pound extends his claim of Jefferson's greatness by pairing him with his other hero, Mussolini. Pound wrote the book in 1933, starting it a month after his meeting with Mussolini. The subtitle is *L'Idea Statale, Fascism as I Have Seen It*, Pound having by then lived in Italy for over eight years. The book is Pound's only statement of his political theories and is his first attempt at a coherent political philosophy, one which encompassed both Jefferson and *il Duce*. Mussolini, however, and not Fascism, is Pound's focus, with Jefferson only a reference to attract American readers. Mussolini is a composite figure for Pound, blending artist, editor and leader, but, most importantly, a man of action who could cut through all obstacles to the core of a problem. So, too, could Jefferson, who would appear repeatedly in Pound's radio broadcasts from Rome made during the early 1940s.

Pound also established in *Eleven New Cantos* the eleven-canto series – what he would call a "decad" – which would become the basic unit of the poem. The first five cantos of this series transpose Venice to America with a focus on the Founding Fathers, the voices of John Adams, Jefferson, John Quincy Adams and their acts of civilizing the New World. But corruption soon takes over through Clay, Calhoun and Webster as venality and exploitative labor practices emerge. But, suddenly and unexpectedly, there is a transition: Canto XXXVI.

This canto is a departure containing Pound's translation of Cavalcanti's "Donna mi prega," offering in lyrical imagery a poised, elegant voice in contrast to combative American voices and vices that precede it. It opens with:

> A lady asks me
> > I speak in season
> > She seeks reason for an affect, wild often
> > That is so proud he hath Love for a name . . .
> Where memory liveth,
> > it takes its state
> Formed like a diafan from light on shade . . .
> > > > (XXXVI/177)

Pound had labored over a translation of this poem for years and its calm intensity here makes it an axis for *Eleven New Cantos* as it shows how love imprints itself on memory. Its psychological intensity separates it from many of the other Cantos but its respite is brief. By Canto XXXVII, one is back in America amid the politics and self-serving businessmen eager to generate the pointless consumption of goods.

Banks and money soon begin to dominate, although satire has its place as when Marconi, the inventor of the radio, has an audience with the Pope and seems to replace him in offering an electronic power of spiritual transmission as radio waves replace beams of divine guidance (XXXVIII/187). The tone is more like *Hugh Selwyn Mauberley*. The final sequence returns to Homer and the original themes of Odysseus traveling to the underworld coupled with metamorphosis, combined in Canto XXXIX. Now, however, Odysseus is hip:

> Fat panther lay by me
> Girls talked there of fucking, beasts talked there of eating,
> All heavy with sleep, fucked girls and fat leopards,
> Lions loggy with Circe's tisane
>
> (XXXIX/193)

"'My bikini is worth your raft'" Leucothea later tells Odysseus in the poem (XCI/636).

Pound thought of *The Cantos* as reconstructing history and he ends *Eleven New Cantos* with precisely that achievement, and even on a note of hope:

> "Ma qvesto,"
> Said the Boss, "è divertente."
> catching the point before the aesthetes had got there.
>
> (XLI/202)

The speaker is Mussolini as Pound recreates his conversation with *il Duce*. Pound had sent a copy of *A Draft of XXX Cantos* to Mussolini who agreed to a brief audience with *il Poeta*. Mussolini told Pound he found *The Cantos* diverting, a remark that impressed Pound. By the end of this Canto, Pound believes that the example of *il Duce* shows how social virtue is overtaking Italy. *Eleven New Cantos* begins with Jefferson and ends with Mussolini. Pound began his prose study, *Jefferson and/or Mussolini*, as he was finishing these Cantos.

In the text of *Eleven Cantos*, Pound introduces the idea of politics as an irregular motion of accents undercutting the prosody of official laws and administrative regulations. He also re-discovers the ideogrammic method, located in the work of Fenollosa. This became a new style which would establish a kind of signifying whole extrapolated from a heap of concrete particulars. It became a kind of model for what was to come in his monumental poem in which language could evoke concrete action. Yet neither the ideogram, Noh drama, nor the fugal method resolved the form of the long poem. The final line of *Eleven New Cantos* is "ad interim 1933" ("in the meantime," or "for the time being," with the date of 1933) (XLI/206). Such incompleteness would never be erased from his work, yet the provisional nature and sense of the improvisational became the very source of its energy.

The *Fifth Decad of Cantos* (1937) and *Cantos LII–LXXI* (1940) quickly followed, texts that opened up the economic references and themes in the work. Monetary reforms become the new focus, expressed through reference to the Monte dei Paschi bank in sixteenth-century Siena, and changes later instigated in eighteenth-century Tuscany by Leopoldo. The history of China and the career of John Adams also become part of the presiding issues. Both volumes focus on the corruption of the West, attributed to usury, a Poundian evil (and the subject of Canto XLV). In these Cantos, he searches for alternate, pre-capitalist systems of exchange, while celebrating the values of Confucians and the ideals of early America.

The *Fifth Decad of Cantos* begins with the Sienese bank, Monte dei Paschi, a symbol of fiscal stability which he elaborates in a section entitled "Banks" in *Social Credit: An Impact* (1935; *SP* 240). This era unites use-value and exchange-value, where use, not speculation, determines worth. Nature, money and people join in what he identifies as a relation of responsibility (XLIII/217). Leopoldine reforms two centuries later continue the value of a central bank to a society and culture (XLIV/223). This prepares one to understand the destructiveness of usury which Pound catalogues in Canto XLV. The following Canto pursues usury in modern times, linking it to war and condemning modern banks which make money "*ex nihil*," out of nothing (XLVI//233).

Mythic and erotic desires which are poetic and creative counter this world of usury, although Canto XLVIII is something of a miscellany, a *pot pourri* of history, domestic memories, the First World War, English history and sacred places of Provence. Calm and order returns with the so-called "Seven Lakes Canto," Canto XLIX, based on a series of paintings and poems of river scenes in a Japanese manuscript book owned by Pound's parents. It underscores a theme of *The Fifth Decad* and the following volume: the seasonal relationship between time and work. Accuracy also becomes a keynote and it is appropriate that Canto LI, which ends the volume, contains the ideograms for Chêng and Ming, the "right name" (LI/252). They recur also at the end of Canto LX/333 and throughout the Adams Cantos, especially LXVI and LXVII. The first of the Chinese Cantos in the following volume repeats the lesson "Call things by the names" (LII/261). A prospective glance ends *The Fifth Decad*; a retrospective view begins *Cantos LII–LXXI*.

A simple bipolar structure fashions *Cantos LII–LXXI*: the first half, Cantos LII–LXI, focus on China; the second, Cantos LXI–LXXI, on John Adams. "Between KUNG and ELEUSIS" (LII/258) announces the union of Confucian management and Greek fertility ceremonies at Eleusis. A Confucian reading of Chinese history and John Adams's revolution in America become sites for the meaningful operation of these concepts. Joining idealistic thought and pragmatic politics is the way Pound protests against modern capitalism's debasement of work. Pound's own effort to research Sienese history is the content of the early Cantos in this section. One must work toward knowledge, not just receive it. Archival work precedes knowledge and Pound's citation of texts shows that they are able to transmit authority and preserve law. Knowledge of the necessary documents makes argument possible – in the case of Adams, knowledge of the British statutes and Coke's *Institutes of the Laws of England* (LXIV/359 and LXXI/419).

For Pound, laws equal the rites and ceremonies of the *Li Ki*, a book of observances and a part of Confucian culture (LII/258–61). "Empire of laws not of men" summarizes Pound's stand on the matter; its source is John Adams (LXVII/391). Law is not subject to "the temper of individuals" but is of "the just middle, the pivot" (LXII/343; LIII/269). This is the Confucian "Unwobbling Pivot" Pound cites in Canto LXX (413) which also upholds the value of documents and the law. Disinterestedness conveyed through the law is essential for the dynastic triumph fundamental for a society.

Adams, not Jefferson, becomes Pound's new hero in the late 1930s, shifting away from the exceptionalism of the individual seen in Odysseus or even Malatesta. Adams appears to provide a greater access to the issues of authority and money which have started to dominate Pound's thinking and writing. Pound was also recognizing at this stage in the poem a stronger sense of his own family history, focusing on his grandfather, Thaddeus Coleman Pound, considered a victim of the coalition of politics and business. From the genius of Jefferson to the administration of Adams is one way to conceptualize the shift in focus of *The Cantos* through the middle part of the poem. Pound stated it succinctly in *Jefferson and/or Mussolini* when he wrote "John Adams believed in heredity. Jefferson left no sons" (*J/M* 19). Adams and the Chinese leaders were similar in that they both accepted the social responsibility of leadership; both understood that the "Good of the empire" is "like a family affair" (LXI/337, 338).

But Pound doesn't end the series until he reasserts the fundamental perversion of use brought about by capital. "Money is not a product of nature but an invention of man," he summarizes (*SP* 316). The statement is from *Gold and Work* published in 1944, in a section headed "The Toxicology of Money." Shifting between the constitutional and revolutionary, covering the reverence for documents and the need to rewrite them in this portion of *The Cantos*, Pound pulls together disparate texts and times as he struggles to make it whole. He also supports the claim that labor is value informed by one's tasks, not time. The struggle between a pre-industrial society and capitalism gives this section of the poem its energy.

Work, labor, value and money are terms that identify the issues of these Cantos embedded in Pound's representation of Confucius and Adams, China and America. Indeed, his co-joining the two cultures establishes a kind of American, or at least republican, aesthetic, demonstrating what one commentator calls "the *American* nature of Pound's modernity – the artist as artisan, workmanlike and constructivist, combining beauty and utility."[8] Nature and technology become one as the natural landscape and modern technology provide the resources for one another. However, it is important to note that Pound wrote *Cantos LII–LXXI* hurriedly – the Adams section in only five weeks – yet he celebrated a vision of ordered government before Europe exploded. He struggled to move to Paradise in the poem, although events would conspire to test his commitment.

Pound began planning the paradisical end of *The Cantos* in 1944, announcing in Canto XLVI that:

> This case, and with it
> the first part, draws to a conclusion,
> of the first phase of this opus
>
> (XLVI/233–4)

He wrote to T. S. Eliot in January 1940 that he had 29 Cantos to write to match Dante's 100 in the *Divine Comedy*. Pound's Fascism and anti-Semitism, however, were making the close difficult, as well as his sudden arrest in May 1945 by Italian partisans. His release and then voluntary appearances at the American forces headquarters led to his imprisonment, ending up at the Disciplinary Training Center just north of Pisa. His original intention was merely to register with the new occupying forces; his arrest was unexpected. During the troubling war years, as he continued to travel to Rome to make inflammatory radio broadcasts to America, and led a more difficult life with Dorothy and Olga, he wrote only fragments and the two so-called "Italian Cantos," LXXII and LXXIII.

During the war, Pound was forced to move with Dorothy to Olga Rudge's small home in Sant'Ambrogio above Rapallo. There, Pound learned that Italy's most important treasures were being destroyed in the mayhem, one of them supposedly the Tempio Malatestiano in Rimini. He was himself almost destroyed by the news and alternated between defiance and impassivity. The former resulted in Cantos LXXII and LXXIII, written in Italian in January and February 1944 and for many years excluded from full, one-volume editions of his poem, until 1985 when they first appeared in Mary de Rachewiltz's bilingual edition of her father's poem. Mussolini's last public speech and the death of the Futurist and Fascist Tomaso Marinetti spurred Pound into writing, choosing Italian as a kind of "*riscossa*" or counter-attack, Mussolini's last cry to his people. Pound had also been translating a selection of his own previous work in Italian since 1943, which made the language an appropriate form of expression for his two new Cantos.

Canto LXXII depicts the return of Marinetti's spirit to ask Pound for his body so that he can continue to fight in the war. Pound demurs and suggests younger men. Two others then come forward, including Ezzelino da Romano, a thirteenth-century Ghibillene whom Dante sees boiling in *Inferno* XII. In Ezzelino's enraged voice, Pound calls for the damnation of Italy's peacemakers and revenge for the destruction of the monuments at Rimini. Canto LXXIII, shorter, represents the exultation of Cavalcanti returned from the world of Venus to witness the "heroism" of a young girl who sacrifices her life by leading Canadian soldiers who had raped her into a minefield (see LXXIII/439, 441).[9] At this stage, the poem began to suffer from what Pound called a "Confusion of voices as from several transmitters, broken phrases" (LXXII/436).

Pound was sent to Pisa after interrogation at Genoa. And after his near-collapse in the steel cage and removal to a tent in the DTC's medical compound, he began to write again. He planned to continue with his translation into English of Confucius' *The Great Digest, The Unwobbling Pivot, The Analects* and *The Classic Anthology*, started in Rapallo. He still had his bilingual edition of the Confucian texts and small Chinese dictionary. Frightened that his physical and perhaps mental breakdown might cause him to lose his memory, he began to write a set of new Cantos in pencil in a notebook which would then be retyped. In this crisis and not knowing his fate, Pound sought the redeeming energy of memory and language. *The Pisan Cantos* were underway.

Recasting some verses originally written in Italian, Pound proceeded to write some of the most autobiographical poetry in *The Cantos*. Nature was the centerpiece, the landscape enlarging his vision of the natural world. History established the context but it is surrounded by nature, the vehicle of light:

> Butterflies, mint and Lesbia's sparrows,
> the voiceless with bumm drum and banners,
> and the ideogram of the guard roosts
>
> (LXXIV/448)

Soon, he reveals more of his past as he becomes self-critical and confessional:

> The ant's a centaur in his dragon world.
> Pull down thy vanity, it is not man
> Made courage, or made order, or made grace,
>   Pull down thy vanity, I say pull down.
> Learn of the green world   (LXXXI/541)

In a "Note to [the] Base Censor," Pound had to explain that his poem contained no secret codes. Interspersed with his memories – partly stimulated by the interrogation he was undergoing by both the military and the FBI – were events at the camp, disrupting the presentation of the past. Diary and reminiscence superimposed themselves on a kind of visionary poetry originating in the immediate. But he needed new models, the totalizing epic of Dante no longer able to contain the irregular flow of experiences. He adopted the lyric and episodic *Testament* of Villon. Textually, the very first lines he wrote at Pisa recall the hanging of Louis Till, a US soldier who committed a crime, and they incorporate Villon's gallows setting. In his imitation of Villon, Pound rejected the hierarchy implicit in Confucius' ordered world and the morality of Dante. The outcast, not the governor, became the new force, the bohemian not the courtier.

Pound had completed a decad of *Pisan Cantos* (Cantos LXXIV–LXXXIV) when he learned in a letter from Dorothy of the death of a promising poet and correspondent, J. P. Angold, and was prompted to compose a coda to the sequence – Canto LXXXIV, an angry farewell to Mussolini and others – but this caused him to reorder ten lines and move them to the opening. The placement of these angry lines at the beginning of *The Pisan Cantos* presents a more political and programmatic section than the one he had previously completed. With this change, *The Pisan Cantos* begin:

> The enormous tragedy of the dream in the peasant's bent shoulders
> Manes! Manes was tanned and stuffed,
> Thus Ben and la Clara *a Milano*
>   by the heels at Milano
> That maggots shd/eat the dead bullock   (LXXIV/445)

But in the final Canto of the series (LXXXIV), there is hope – "Under white clouds, cielo di Pisa / out of all this beauty something must come" (559) – which the concluding lines re-confirm: "If the hoar frost grip thy tent / Thou wilt give thanks when night is spent" (LXXXIV/560). *The Pisan Cantos* both resists and employs the lyrical, supported by the visionary association with forms of personal redemption through reclamation of the past. Compassion emerges, as a search for an imagined but redefined future occurs:

> Le Paradis n'est pas artificiel
>   but spezzato apparently
>   it exists only in fragments unexpected excellent sausage,
>   the smell of mint, for example
>   (LXXIV/458)

Memory is the mode Pound follows. Without texts, a library or other resources, he relies on what he remembers, on one hand establishing a kind of associative logic and on the other creating lapses and gaps. More important, perhaps, the act of recreation stimulates a review of his past that often condenses action as in this passage from Canto LXXX/520:

> so that leaving America I brought with me $80
>   and England a letter of Thomas Hardy's
>   and Italy one eucalyptus pip
> from the salita that goes up from Rapallo
>   (if I go)

The first line refers to his 1908 departure from America and arrival at Gibraltar; the second, his 1920 departure from England with a letter from Thomas Hardy on "Propertius"; the third mentions a seed he picked up as he was marched away from Sant'Ambrogio by Italian partisans when arrested on 3 May 1945.

But do the *The Pisan Cantos* mark Pound's repentance? Does he recant his Fascism and racism or are they a lament for a movement's passing? No clear answer exists because, throughout the sequence, Pound's aesthetic and ideology contrast. A new confessional mode overrides all:

>   nothing matters but the quality
>   of the affection –
>   in the end – that has carved the trace in the mind
>   dove sta memoria   (LXXVI/477)

With the Malatesta and, perhaps, Chinese Cantos, *The Pisan Cantos* are the most sustained and successful series in the entire long poem. Pound, himself, sensed this when he wrote to Dorothy that "the new Cantos are simpler in parts [and] there is a certain amount of new technique" (*LC* 137). Their winning the Bollingen Prize for Poetry offered by the Library of Congress in 1949 confirmed their importance, although also intensified the criticism leveled against him.

Three other volumes would follow to complete *The Cantos*. The first was the unusually titled *Section: Rock-Drill de los cantares: LXXXV–XCV* (1955). Written largely at St. Elizabeths where Pound was incarcerated after his trial in Washington, the poems resurrect ideas he formulated in 1940, essentially the conflict between "the usurer and any man who / wants to do a good job" (LXXXVII/589). The odd title actually refers to an expressionistic sculpture composed of harsh planes by Jacob Epstein, an American-born British sculptor Pound greatly admired: *Rock Drill* (1913–15), done with intersecting planes and edges, linking motion and machinery. The fascinating and controversial work had a futuristic figure wearing a visored helmet attached to an angular neck and a machined body poised on a tripod over a phallic mechanical drill pointed earthward. Man dehumanized into a machine was the image, the armored and mechanized figure obscuring any sense of the human.

Rock Drill, the sculpture, was exhibited at the London Group in March 1915 and challenged viewers to accept a real machine, the drill, as a legitimate part of art, as well as the representation of a human being as a machine. Intensifying the crude realism of the machinery, as several critics noted, was that the drill was American made. Yet the issue for many became the incongruity between the insistent and exposed detail of the engine with the synthetic form of man. Not, however, for Pound who admired the work, insisting in 1916 that when machinery is expressive of efficiency it can be beautiful, although such beauty is often offensive to the school of "sentimental aesthetics" (*GB* 17). Later, he would write that the beauty of machines is to be found "where the energy is most concentrated" (*MAO* 57).

In form and structure, *Rock-Drill* parallels *The Fifth Decad* in that the first five cantos contrast with the following six. The turn in this volume is the poet's reinvigoration through his relationship with Sheri Martinelli, although the style and metric differ from anything else in *The Cantos*. The expression is terse and elliptical in its references. Nothing seems ordered, yet everything is ordered. Canto LXXXV, for example, contains a selective treatment of Chinese history going beyond the chronological recital of the Chinese Cantos, LII–LXI. The principles of good governance are reduced to outline form, interspersed with a panoply of people and incidents from European history. References are often opaque, however. Everything, it seems, is abbreviated, so that allusions to the death of Mussolini, the execution of Mary Surratt as an accomplice in the assassination of Lincoln (despite testimony by John Holohan), and the history of juries, all condense in the lines that end the canto:

> Dead in the Piazzale Loreto,
> In Holohan's case, murder protected.
> Jury trial was in Athens.
> Tyrants resisted   (LXXXV/579)

The Canto and, indeed, volume also exhibit more extravagant Chinese ideograms. Later Cantos in the book deal with banking in America, with appropriate heroes and villains ending the series with Canto LXXXIX juxtaposing historical Chinese protagonists with those in early America, plus classical Athens and nineteenth-century Washington.

Cantos XC–XCIII are by contrast focused on love and a return to light, associated with Sheri Martinelli, a former model, painter, eccentric and visitor of Pound's at St. Elizabeths. She appears mythically in the poems associated with Sibylla-Beatrice, Kuthera (Aphrodite), Ra-Set, Leucothea and Undine. She is an idealized woman associated with understanding and poetic inspiration. Richard St. Victor, an early Church Father, also appears, as well as obscure philosophers. However, Pound updates myth, having Leucothea appear in a bikini, not a veil, when rescuing Odysseus (XCI, XCVIII) – the clothing associated with a photo Martinelli had taken of herself in a mirror wearing a bikini (a photo verified by H. D.: *END* 52).

All of these allusions are to invoke the druid-like or at least mythical actions of Pound and Martinelli at St. Elizabeths where they burned incense on a small stone on the lawn and imagined a vision of a classical altar of which Pound made a sketch that was to appear in Canto XC. References to Martinelli, "a spirit in cloth of Gold" (Canto XCI/635), reoccur in Cantos CIV, CVI and CXI. Repetition of "*m'elevasti*" ("you lifted me up") throughout the series suggest the impact of Martinelli on Pound (XC/626). The final two Cantos in *Rock-Drill* (XCIV and XCV) unite spiritual love and its manifestation in nature with public/political heroes and social order, although earlier Pound celebrated the link between light and love:

> Trees die & the dream remains
>> Not love but that love flows from it
>> ex animo
>> & cannot ergo delight in itself
>> but only in the love flowing from it.
> UBI AMOR IBI OCULUS EST.
>
>   (XC/629)

Translated, the final line from Richard St. Victor reads "Where love is, there is the eye." Pound gravitates to the condition where "the crystal wave mount to flood surge" (XCV/664).

Thrones de los Cantares XCVI–CIX (1959) is next. Written at St. Elizabeths, the poems struggle between Pound's desire for pedagogical directness and use of recondite references. The poems often jumble forms, prose mixing with ideograms and verse, with various asides rationalizing his method. On p. 679, for example, he clearly writes that:

> *If we never write anything save what is already*
> *understood, the field of understanding will never be*
> *extended. One demands the right, now and again,*
> *to write for a few people with special interests*
> *and whose curiosity reaches into greater detail.*
>
> (XCVI/679)

On the other hand, an entire verse paragraph in Latin from Migne's *Patrologia* stands in stark need of a translation and context. Greek, both modern and ancient, contests for a kind of linguistic supremacy with Latin, while ideograms and English do battle. An imperious tone dominates the volume, as though only an elect few could decipher the erudite references.

Thrones seems remote from the world as Pound turns in on himself, a metaphoric expression of his isolation at St. Elizabeths in the center of the nation's capital. A kind of secret history seems to be written in these lines which many critics have deemed unreadable. Hermetic, they resist openings. The descent into darkness by Leucothea which opens Canto XCVI, having saved Odysseus by giving him her veil (in this case her bikini), introduces Pound's own descent at St. Elizabeths. Visionary insight versus civic wisdom could summarize the conflicts that follow, however. An eighth-century history by Paul the Deacon becomes a source text for his representation of what he outlined as thrones in Dante's *Paradiso*, as he explained to the poet Donald Hall in 1960. The Dantean thrones

> are for the spirits of the people who have been responsible for good
> government. The thrones in the Cantos are an attempt to move out from
> egoism and to establish some definition of an order possible or at any
> rate conceivable on earth.[10]

Byzantium is the first example of such order because for Pound it exemplified the codification of Roman law. It is a place that will remain in his imagination through the final volume, *Drafts & Fragments*.

This complex sequence exhibits a gap between the mass of local detail and the abstract principle for which it stands. Twisted phrases and syntax work against Pound's desire to get his ideas across cleanly and directly. To illustrate his predicament of a predicated secrecy, Pound cites Lenin: "Aesopian language (under censorship) / where I wrote 'Japan' you may read 'Russia'" (C/733). Yet the situation is ironic, since Pound still claims that "Precise terminology is the first implement" (XCIX/731). He revivifies his commitment to the local, declaring that "Harmony is in the proportion of branches / as clarity" and that "The plan is in nature / rooted" (XCIX/728, 729). But yet overall, *Thrones* confirms the failure of coherence to bind the poem, at one time Pound's hope. Nevertheless, there is a return, in the final two Cantos, to American and European history before intersecting voices almost drown the poet's sound (CIX/794).

Drafts & Fragments (1969) concludes, but does not end, the poem. Published as a separate text in 1968–9, two years before its inclusion in the entire *Cantos*, it has always been the object of debate because there is no single text. Ostensibly, it begins with Canto CX, but its termination is unclear: various editions shift between "CXVI" or "Notes for CXVII et seq." More recent editions conclude with "Fragments (1966)" which is a celebration of Olga Rudge.

The difficulty, in part, was that Pound felt nothing he wrote after *Thrones* was in a form sufficiently good to be published. Having sent Donald Hall, who interviewed him in 1962, portions of supposed Cantos CX–CXVI, the material found its way into a pirated edition published by Fuck You / Press, a mimeographed work titled *Cantos 110–116*. Between 1962 and 1967, Pound published other versions of these poems in various journals. James Laughlin, through New Directions, immediately responded to the 1967 pirated edition by preparing a New Directions volume entitled *Drafts & Fragments*, so titled to reflect the unfinished nature of the poems. But by this time, Pound was ill and not participating in the editorial process. Creating closure for the large poem had proven both difficult and elusive; indeed, the principles of Imagism and Vorticism were opposed to such a notion. However, the New Directions volume did appear and was incorporated in the 1970 printing of the complete poem.

One of the most controversial texts was Canto "CXX" which appeared in a journal in 1970. Included in the 1972 New Directions edition of *The Cantos*, it is a work that asks forgiveness:

> Let the Gods forgive what I
> have made
> Let those I love try to forgive
> what I have made.

However, after various textual placements, the passage was removed from its terminal spot in 1981 and placed among the "CXVII et seq." section on p. 822, now titled "Notes for CXVII et seq." This text, however, fashions a contrite end to a politically charged poem, failing to achieve a paradisical close of even fragmentary resolution to a work that questioned coherence. Culture, at least in Europe, also seems to have come to an end: "and the European mind stops," Pound laments in CXV/ 814.

Textual instability is everywhere, even though Pound still manages to render – in moments – a paradise of natural harmony. But self-doubt and disharmony reduce the complex inter-textuality that characterizes so much of the poem. As he writes in CXVI,

> the beauty is not the madness
> Tho' my errors and wrecks lie about me.
> And I am not a demigod,
> I cannot make it cohere.
> If love be not in the house there is nothing.

"Many errors, / a little rightness" he states, adding "I cannot make it flow thru" (CXVI/ 815–16, 817).

Pound did show, however, that poetry could be made from pieces – what he called "gists and piths," a definition of poetry found in a footnote on page 92 of the *ABC of Reading*. His mature work celebrates poetry as an arrangement of rough, juxtaposed elements; coherent or integrated wholes he distrusts (*ABCR* 92). However, the flints sometime seem arbitrary, as in Canto XLVIII, a miscellany without order. The splicing of anecdote, scraps of reading, mythic invention, a letter from his daughter, whirl together. His condensation makes him at times cryptic, while the excision of rhetoric challenges readers of the entire poem. This poetry of reticence finds its voice not in the poet's self but history, in allusion and the sound of others who speak in the poem to offset a kind of "purism of surface and form."[11] The fragmented form, however, became influential for the next generation of modernists, one of the most original being William S. Burroughs. His "cut-ups," texts made from slicing typewritten text into fragments and then re-arranging them into a new narrative, derives partly from Pound's work (recall CX /801: "From time's wreckage shored, / these fragments shored against ruin"). The LANGUAGE POETS also applied the "gists and piths" technique of Pound.

Throughout the later Cantos, Pound became increasingly conscious of the visual dimensions of text, incorporating a series of images ranging from the musical score that makes up all of Canto LXXV to the Chinese ideograms that appear with growing frequency; XCIV/656 is a page almost entirely of ideograms. At the end of Canto LXXXVIII/609, the heart, diamond, clubs and spades from a set of playing cards stand alone as signs of meaning divorced from language. Earlier, Pound actually reproduced literal signs as in LXXI/418 which reads:

JOHN ADAMS
FOR PEACE
1800

An Egyptian hieroglyph appears in XCIII at p. 647. Adding to the distinctiveness of the visual in the poem is dialect. At unexpected moments, the voices in the poem speak in a dialect that is distinctly presented on the page and may be equally American regional or foreign, supplemented with unorthodox spelling, which he would so often use in his letters.

Collections of *The Cantos* first appeared in deluxe editions: William Bird's Three Mountains Press published *A Draft of XVI. Cantos* in Paris in 1925; *A Draft of The Cantos 17–27* appeared in London through John Rodker in 1928, while Nancy Cunard printed *A Draft of XXX Cantos* in Paris in 1930. The use of "draft" in each title suggests the provisional nature of his "Poem of Some Length." His choice of this exclusive and expensive form of publication, the first two volumes with beautifully illustrated capitals, the third exquisitely handset and produced on expensive paper with linen boards and, again, ornate initials, suggests an elite readership. The modern was for the privileged. Only after 1933 did Pound begin to publish with more mainstream publishers, with the aim of having his poem read rather than collected. Importantly, Pound carefully oversaw the production of these deluxe editions, even finding a master printer in Paris for Nancy Cunard's edition and participating in the choice of font size and design.

The appearance of the first thirty Cantos in ornate, deluxe editions increased their desirability as works of art if not as literary texts. Although they were "trial settings" of his poem, drafts, Pound saw no contradiction in their publication in rich, seemingly permanent material form. The display of text, although still evolving, was as much the centerpiece as the content. As Pound made clear in a letter of 1939, "all typographic disposition, placings of words *on* the page, is intended to facilitate the reader's intonation, whether he be reading silently to self or aloud to friends. Given time and technique I might even put down the musical notation of passages or 'breaks into song'" (*SL* 322).

In the 1920s in Cantos VIII–XI, Pound incorporated the exploits of Sigismondo Malatesta and the rivalries of Italian states. In the 1930s Pound sought another form of Renaissance, that of Vorticism, and shortly after the publication of *A Draft of XXX Cantos* commissioned a translation of his article "Vorticism" into Italian. He wanted to transmit the Vorticist ideals into the terms of the new Italy. Economic concerns and hero worship contributed in equal doses to Pound's celebration of Mussolini, but the hope of a reinvigorated Vorticism also had a role. What he wanted to test was whether or not Vorticism could effect political change. Earlier, in 1914, the movement had failed to initiate any social or political revolution. Now, in the mid 1930s, Vorticism seemed to color Pound's arguments for Fascism, one sign of its renewed effectiveness being the argument of Wyndham Lewis in his 1934 essay "Plain Home-Builder: Where is Your Vorticist?" In this essay, Lewis admits that twenty years earlier the war had interfered with the Vorticist program of social reform and that "in the heat of this pioneer action we were even inclined to forget *the picture* altogether in favor of *the frame*."[12] But then, as now, he and others were making blueprints for a new civilization. With Mussolini, it now seemed possible. The "clean line" applied to both Vorticism and Fascism: the control and aggression fostered in the Vorticist aesthetic expressed by geometric gestures found full expression in Mussolini's government and control.

Prose

Once Pound began *The Cantos*, he wrote almost no occasional poetry; no lyrics, sonnets or any other verse of value appeared, except what went into his long poem. His energies were directed toward *The Cantos* or a series of prose works that mixed personal opinions with literary analysis, musical commentary, economic history and social criticism: *Gaudier-Brzeska, A Memoir* (1916), *Pavannes and Divisions* (1918), *Instigations . . . Together with an Essay on the Chinese Written Character* (1920), *Antheil and the Treatise on Harmony* (1924), *How to Read* (1931), *ABC of Economics* (1933), *ABC of Reading* (1934), *Make It New* (1934), *Jefferson and/or Mussolini* (1935), *Social Credit: An Impact* (1935), *Polite Essays* (1937), *Guide to Kulchur* (1938) and *Literary Essays* (ed. T. S. Eliot, 1954).

Several titles stand out: the programmatic *ABC of Reading*, filled with Poundian directives on what and how to read; *Guide to Kulchur* (1938), an encyclopedic view of past and present cultures; and *Literary Essays*, edited by T. S. Eliot. This last is a provocative sampling of the range of Pound's literary criticism. *Make It New* of 1934 caught the eye of Samuel Beckett who, in his review of the book, noted its variegated but linked subjects, stating that "in sum a galvanic belt of essays, education by provocation, Spartan maieutics."[13] Pound's valuable *Gaudier-Brzeska* anticipates a number of the points made in the collection of critical essays.

Not surprisingly, Pound's prose often took shape as a manifesto, whether it is the early "A Few Don'ts by an Imagiste" (1913), "National Culture, A Manifesto 1938" or his pamphlet *What is Money For?* (1939). The declaratory tone and insistent attitude of the manifesto, plus its unusual announcement of something new, perfectly suited Pound who, from early in his writing career, expanded the American tradition of the jeremiad, the prose invective lamenting the current social state, challenging an impending decline through an exhortation to action. In 1909, Marinetti published the first of his Futurist manifestos, showing how the form, adopted from the political sphere, could work in the artistic world. T. H. Hulme's lecture "Romanticism and Classicism" (1912) was another manifesto, calling for a new hardness and clarity in writing. The goal was explicitly the refutation of explanatory excess and of the metrical predictability of nineteenth-century writing.

Pound himself would, naturally, issue many manifestos: on Imagism, Vorticism, history and economics. Radical ideas meant to shock, startle and awake readers were standard and often expressed in arresting, violent typography that equaled their outlandish positions. The 1914 manifesto of BLAST thunders "**BLAST** / years **1837** to **1900**" – that is, damn the Victorians. The Vorticist principle of dynamic content replaced the laconic-ness of Imagism. Another manifesto of the period is Mina Loy's "Feminist Manifesto" of 1914, which, like BLAST, manipulated words for maximum effect. It opens with a clear-cut statement:

> The feminist movement as at present instituted is
> Inadequate

Later, she challenges the cliché that woman is the equal of man. She is not, she emphasizes, and advises that women

> Leave off looking to men to find out what you are not – seek
> within yourselves to find out what you are[14]

No group, it seems, could do without a manifesto. The Dadaists, Surrealists, Expressionists and Cubists had them. The rhetoric and tone of the "genre" infuse Pound's prose, offering and re-offering clear, if not extreme, statements of new ideas.

Several consistent ideas emerge in Pound's prose, although it would be false to imagine a uniform set of concepts; rather, they form a kind of intellectual journal expressing an emerging poetic. His letters, in fact, contain in miniature his larger principles as the following sentences highlight:

> A revelation is always didactic.   (*SL* 180)

> If the poets don't make certain horrors appear horrible who will?
>
> (*SL* 181)

> The more a man goes over a real writer the more he know that *no reader*
> ever read anything the first time he saw it. . .   (*SL* 287)

But is there a Poundian aesthetic? Yes, and its formulation might be "the touchstone of an art is its precision" (*LE* 48). It begins with the need to know well selected great works of world literature, through knowledge of a limited number of outstanding texts. Next would be a commitment to write concisely and concretely, resisting the idea of poetry as an abstraction, preferring the terms of technical language found in mathematics or physics.

Pound also avoids biographical criticism, focusing almost exclusively on the texts themselves, preferring an indirect method which in his later critical books often consists of excerpts from essential texts, works he felt were fundamental to an understanding of literature. In the early 1940s, during his friendship with the philosopher George Santayana, then retired to Italy, he prepared a document in Italian entitled *Estetica pragmatica di E. P.*, translated as "Pragmatic Aesthetics". The adjective was to represent "function" and applied to his Fenollosian view of disengaging writing from grammar (which he associated with logic). Poetry was to be more in accord with science, which in the *ABC of Reading* he identified as the method of detail and the particular. Pound tried to rescue writing from metaphysics.

As early as the 1910s, Pound considered the relationship of literature to science. This approach, along with his essay "Machine Art," places aesthetics in the sphere of the practical. Vorticism is the prelude to his idea of mechanical function, or the coinciding of beauty with function. Form is important only to the degree it carries out a function. "Machine Art" criticizes the subjective in art, expanding the imperative of Imagism to depersonalize art. Pound was updating the notion of the *technê*, the Greek term used by Aristotle to imply art as a ruled skill in making something. Art *is* a set of rules, a skill in making. In Greek, the term implies both a technical *and* artistic ability. To this Pound adds functionalism: "we find a thing beautiful in proportion to its aptitude to a function" (*MAO*, 18). Art for Pound, then, becomes the skill of making, and beauty is aptness for purpose. Canto LXXXV from *Rock-Drill* summarizes this when he writes

$\frac{1}{2}$ research   and $\frac{1}{2}$ Technê
$\frac{1}{2}$ observation, $\frac{1}{2}$ Technê
$\frac{1}{2}$ training, $\frac{1}{2}$ Technê

(LXXXV/ 570. Pound provides the original Greek for Technê.)

Interestingly, the new craftsman for Pound is the engineer, not the architect. Art for Pound has become – no, it always was – something practical and useful, as he outlined in "How to Read" (1929). "Pragmatic Aesthetics" repeats Pound's earlier aesthetic which focused on the exact. As he summarizes, "true thinking is ideogrammic in the sense that the general is composed of *definite particulars known directly* by the thinker" (*MAO* 158). But he never forgets that "great literature is simply language charged with meaning to the utmost possible degree" (*ABCR* 36).

"Paideuma" is another important concept in Pound's critical thinking, a term coined by the German ethnologist Leo Frobenius. It implies the idea of culture as a *Gestalt*, a kind of living organism where every element is influenced by other elements. For Pound, this is the union of religion, thinking and language, as he outlined in an essay entitled "European Paideuma." In *Guide to Kulchur* (1938), Pound defines it as "the tangle or complex of the inrooted ideas of any period" (*GK* 57). He links the idea to his effort to renovate language, the purpose of *Guide to Kulchur*, where the term is descriptive of an illuminating energy of intellectual perception and understanding inimical to the inductive method. Frobenius meant something to Pound because his ideas of cultural history derived from field work not abstractions. Frobenius appears five times in *The Cantos*, most importantly in bringing "the living fact to bear on the study of dead documents" (*EPE* 212).

One of the most interesting features of Pound's prose is that his style remained consistent. Following the uneven tone of his first book, *The Spirit of Romance*, where the the pull to Edwardian "appreciations" rather than objective criticism reigned, he turned to a clear, direct and hortatory style, evident in his letters even before his criticism. There, he immediately grabbed his correspondent's attention as he would do the reader's and rarely let up, often recognizing that his drive to get his ideas across would override a felicitous style: "my prose is bad," he told Harriet Monroe, "but on ne peut pas pontifier and have style simultaneously" (*SL* 14). He justified this partly because it was necessary to be insistent: "I am perhaps didactic . . . [but] it's all rubbish to pretend that art isn't didactic" (*SL* 180).

Later, to Harriet Monroe again, he would be more characteristically direct: "'They,' the American brood, have ears like elephants and no sense of the English language" (*SL* 15). To Iris Barry he declared, "Really one DON' T need to know a language. One NEEDS, damn well needs, to know the few hundred words in the few really good poems that any language has in it" (*SL* 93). Earlier, he simplified poetry for her into two precepts:

a. concision, or style, or saying what you mean in the fewest and clearest words.
b. the actual necessity for creating or constructing something; of presenting an image, or enough images of concrete things arranged to stir the reader.

(*SL* 90)

Pound did, however, use his letters to experiment with a kind of phonetic dialect, partly for emphasis and partly for attention. Many of his letters to Williams, Bunting, Zukofsky and even James Laughlin exhibit this quality. A single example from a 31 December 1933 letter to the young Laughlin begins with

> DILECTUS FILIUS ["BELOVED SON"]
> (or wotever the god damn vocative may be.)
> Signed on yester day a/m/ with Routledge of LONDON for a tex book
> on licherchoor \
> one up again for the deCAY dent Britons / as being more alert than the
> smart yankee publishers.
> God DAMN an GODDAMMMMMMMMMM!!!!
> Houghton Snifflij [Mifflin] . . . are the bastuds that have printed all the
> safe and tranquil poems of H. D. Get cousin Henry [Laughlin] to poison
> the stinking lot . . .
>
> (*EP/JL* 12)

The loose, almost rollicking style, characterized by unusual spellings and constructions, represents Pound's sense of vocalizing language. Words are, first, sounds through which meaning emerges, while his free-flowing syntax expresses an exuberant but critical mind.

Pound's critical ideas, concisely expressed in his *Selected Letters, 1907–1914*, find further expansion in a series of individual editions, ranging from exchanges with John Quinn, Margaret Cravens, Ford Madox Ford, Joyce, Wyndham Lewis and Louis Zukofsky to those with William Carlos Williams and James Laughlin. These works all contain crucial passages outlining Pound's aesthetic, political and economic views and reiterate his fundamental concept that "art is the particular declaration that *implies* the general; and being particular may not divert . . . melt and muddle like an abstract declaration" (*MAO* 158). But throughout his letters, *aperçus*, directives, suggestions and directions appear with cogency. "Against the metric pattern struggle toward natural speech. You haven't *yet* got sense of quantity," he advises the young Mary Barnard (*SL* 261). "Good editing, as I see it, means the most effective presentation of the best of *whatever* is on hand" he tells Harriet Monroe, although later he would be more direct: "the writer provides the ammunition and the editor shoots it *toward* his target" (*SL* 232, 306); "Excuse this firmness, but hang it, anything else wd. be waste of both our time" (*SL* 272); "Who makes the living line must SWEAT, be gheez!" (*SL* 274).

Pound carried over the directness – but not the phonetic spelling – of his letters to his prose writing. In *ABC of Reading*, for example, he asserts, and commands, and orders the reader to follow certain rules or programs of study, always linked to the individual, including himself: "The critic who doesn't make a personal statement, *in re* measurements he himself has made, is merely an unreliable critic," he announced (*ABCR* 30). There is no time for equivocation, giving his critical statements an urgency as well as an imperious tone: "A general statement is valuable only in REFERENCE to the known objects or facts"; "literature is language charged with meaning" (*ABCR* 26, 28). Extending this directness are lists of titles and authors one should study – lists being his short-hand way of establishing a canon. Or, as he proclaims, "my lists are a starting-point and a challenge" (*ABCR* 43). "READ the best you can find," he admonishes the reader, simply, directly setting out his curriculum for a literary education. In *The Cantos* he frequently confirms these precepts, as in "Precise terminology is the first implement, / dish and container" (XCIX/731).

Pound was also a significant anthologist, beginning with *Des Imagistes* of 1914 which introduced Imagist poetry to readers. He continued with a series of works that allowed him to publicize contemporary poets he liked and demonstrated his critical values. In 1915, he published the *Catholic Anthology*, compiled in part to publish Eliot's "Love Song of J. Alfred Prufrock," although it also included work by Yeats, Williams, Edgar Lee Masters and Carl Sandburg. Dorothy Shakespear designed the cover in a Vorticist style. After a hiatus, he published *Profile* in Italy with the Milanese publisher Giovanni Scheiwiller in 1932. This was a collection of poems, as he phrased it, that stayed in his memory, and included work by T. S. Eliot, Basil Bunting, Ernest Hemingway, Mina Loy, Arthur Symons and others. The year 1933 three saw *Active Anthology* published by Faber and Faber in England. Its intent was to present a series of new poets such as Louis Zukofsky and George Oppen and give some credibility to what would be known as Objectivism. Work by T. S. Eliot, Marianne Moore and e. e. cummings also appeared in it.

Even some of Pound's critical books such as his *ABC of Reading* (1934) could be considered anthologies. Excerpts, which Pound calls "Exhibits," make up almost half the book and they range widely among his favorites – Dante, Cavalcanti, Villon, Yeats – and from the Anglo-Saxon author of "The Wanderer" to Chaucer, the sixteenth-century translator Gavin Davis (the Renaissance translator of Ovid), Arthur Golding, John Donne, Robert Herrick, the Earl of Rochester, the seventeeth-century Samuel Butler, Pope, Crabbe, Landor and, finally, Browning and Whitman. A "Treatise on Metre" completes the volume.

Another anthology of this period is *New Directions in Poetry and Prose* which appeared in 1936. The publisher was James Laughlin who, heeding Pound's direction to give up poetry and do something useful, began a publishing company. His first volume, this anthology, included Pound's Canto XLIV and work by Williams, Stein, e. e. cummings and Marianne Moore. New Directions was born; the first book Pound published with their colophon, appropriately drawn by Gaudier-Brzeska, was *Culture* (1938), the American version of *Guide to Kulchur*, the title of the British edition. New Directions kept all of Pound's books in print throughout his life, an extraordinary commitment since sales were irregular.

Pound's translation of Confucian odes resulted in another anthology. He worked on the texts during and immediately after the war, while also writing *The Pisan Cantos*. He completed the odes in 1949, although they did not appear until 1954 – a compilation of Chinese songs, hymns, and lyrics supposedly selected by Confucius and set to music by him. Pound titled his version *The Classic Anthology as Defined by Confucius*. An accessible work showing how he could convey a distant culture to the present, it remains one of his more practical texts. Synthesizing the colloquial and poetical, he captures the unique voice of each ode, as in this slangy extract from a song of Cheng:

> Hep-Cat Chung, don't jump my wall
> Nor strip my mulberry boughs,
> The boughs don't matter
> But my brothers' clatter!
> > Have a heart, Chung,
> > > It's awful
> > (*CAD* 38)

Confucius to Cummings is a 1964 gathering published by New Directions. It was assembled with Marcella Spann, another Pound acolyte, while Pound was in St. Elizabeths. The wide-ranging list of nearly 100 poems from the ancient world to the modern was intended for classroom use and has a "section for instructors" at the end. Spann wrote the "Preface." A number of the works are Pound's own translations, with an emphasis on Greek, Latin, Chinese, Troubadour, Renaissance and Elizabethan texts. Pound provided notes on selected texts and poets, and a short passage from Canto LIX on the importance of affect generated by poetry – "virtu in internals / Ut animum nostrum purget" ["for the cleansing of the soul"] – ends the "Preface," although Pound then contributed a two-page introduction telling the reader where to start and how to use the book: "begin with cummings or Whitman and read what you like" (*CC* ix).

Pound then criticizes the laziness of English metrists, introduces the term "paideuma" (no doubt surprising for students) and praises Arthur Golding's translation of Ovid. Appendix I contains Pound's note on Thomas Hardy and Ford Madox Ford "who refused the imagist rock-drill." Pound also cogently declares that the "most important critical act of the half-century was in the limpidity of natural speech, driven toward the just word," a condensed summary of his own goals (*CC* 327). The note also contains important details about Pound and his poetic quests and reiterates his determination to combat "the rising tide of imprecision" (*CC* 329). Appendix V contains selections from Pound's criticism chosen by Marcella Spann, largely from the *ABC of Reading*.

By the 1930s, Pound's attraction to economics was greater than his understanding and its pull stronger than that of literature. Introduced to Major C. H. Douglas's ideas on Social Credit through A. R. Orage in 1918, Pound's writing on the topic remained relatively dormant until 1931. After that date, *The Cantos* began to serve his economic and political agenda rather than merely be informed by it. The Depression may have accelerated this interest, coupled with the visible proof of Mussolini's skill in revitalizing Italy's economic growth. His insistence became endemic: "Naturally history without monetary intelligence is mere twaddle" is only one of hundreds of aphorisms which his letters and other writings contain. For a period of time, he preferred to sign his surname with the Pound sign, £ (*SL* 336).

Pound's favored economic historians began with A. R. Orage and *New Age*. This radical left-wing journal with its Fabian and Guild Socialists introduced him to the integration of art and politics, expressed by Orage's adage, "economic power precedes political power" (in Redman, *CCEP* 252). Pound's education in economics was simultaneous with his education in politics. The First World War shattered his belief in a strictly aesthetic valuation of art, which the death of Gaudier-Brzeska in battle further unraveled. His 1918 introduction to Major C. H. Douglas and his ideas of Social Credit altered Pound's attitude toward an isolationist view of art even more, which his review of Douglas and Orage's *Credit Power and Democracy* in *Contact* (1921) confirmed.

Initially, Pound sought to investigate the causes of war in an effort to oppose it. Douglas offered one explanation, as his book *Economic Democracy*, serialized in the *New Age*, showed. Essentially, he believed that an inadequate supply of money and overproduction of goods led to periods of depression which only war and the high demand for produced goods could overcome. This view challenges the law of supply and demand which essentially states that manufacturing a good or delivery of a service produces or places into circulation enough money, through costs and wages, to enable people to purchase the goods and services produced; in other words, supply creates its own demand. Canto XXII/101–2 confirms this challenge through a conversation between Douglas and his opponent John Maynard Keynes.

To counter the capitalist need for profit, making it impossible for markets to clear themselves, which led to dumping and layoffs, trade wars and depressions, Douglas believed additional money had to be introduced. Douglas proposed this would occur through the payment of an annual Social Credit dividend to all citizens. Pound explained the system in Canto XXXVIII/190, describing how the state (Great Britain) created credit by simply printing more money, although war was the only undertaking, it seemed, in which the government was prepared to go into debt. Economic reform was the only way to avoid war, Pound believed.

Although Pound moved to Paris in 1921, he also began to travel extensively in Italy and moved there permanently in 1925, leasing a seafront apartment at 12 via Marsala in Rapallo. His concerns at the time were political, although not those of Mussolini: passports, which he considered a terrible nuisance; United States copyright laws, especially the failure of the US to sign the Berne Convention; and article 211 of the US Penal Code which confused "smutty postcards, condoms, and Catullus" (*EP/BC* 38). Three events, however, drove Pound back to economics: the Depression of 1929 and its international repercussions; the return of A. R. Orage who had quit the *New Age* in 1922 but in 1932 founded the *New English Weekly*, with Pound again contributing economic and political essays; and his meeting with Mussolini on 30 January 1933.

Olga Rudge had given a private concert for *il Duce* in February 1927 and was impressed with the charismatic Italian leader. Pound, who had sent the leader *Draft of XXX Cantos*, was overwhelmed by Mussolini's charm and intelligence when they met in Rome at the Palazzo Venezia, Mussolini greeting him behind a large desk in the Mappamondo chamber. His meeting with him was reported on the front page of the Rapallo paper and the impact was so great that Pound immediately began two new books: *The ABC of Economics* and *Jefferson and/or Mussolini*.

After Douglas, Silvio Gesell was the economist most important for Pound – Gesell being a disciple of Proudhon. *The Natural Economic Order* (1906) was in its seventh edition by 1929 and advocated the quantity theory of money, which argued that money should be issued by the state according to needs and the productive capacity of the nation. Pound first heard of Gesell when he learned of a monetary experiment in Woergl in Austria where, to counteract the effects of the Depression, the mayor issued a village script according to Gesell's idea of stamp script, in which you added a stamp equal to 1% of the note's value each month to maintain that value. The Austrian National Bank soon put an end to the practice, however. Nonetheless, Pound liked the practicality of the system and urged Douglas to incorporate it into his Social Credit scheme.

He resisted but Pound continued to support Gesell's ideas, especially the belief that monetary reform would bring social reform.

Odon Por, a Hungarian, was the next to influence Pound's economic thinking. Por had lived in London since 1912 but would not meet Pound until the thirties. He had also contributed to Orage's the *New Age* and described himself as a "Syndicalist. Guild Socialist. NOT fascist. Free lance" (*CCEP* 258). A prolific political writer, he wrote for various Fascist journals and later made contacts for Pound which eventually led to his appearing on Rome radio. Through extensive correspondence, Por convinced Pound that Mussolini's regime was on its way to adopting Social Credit policies. Confucius was also an influence as Pound believed increasingly that Confucian philosophy and economic reform would bring about an enduring social order.

Pound's method of economic study parallels his method of literary study: a combination of establishing valid contemporary principles and definitions, and then going back into history to find similar insights or examples. In *Social Credit: An Impact* (1935), he clearly outlines his process:

> We need in economics:
> 1. Simplification of terminology;
> 2. Articulation of terminology ("distinguish the root from the branch")
>   We need:
> 3. Less intolerance towards converging movements;
> 4. To hammer on root ideas
>
> (*SC* 13)

Confucius and Dante are the origin of points 1 and 2, the quote coming from the *Ta Hio*. Point 3 is a basic Poundian concern in the thirties: that one's understanding of economics had to be translated into governmental policy. Point 4 expresses his belief that the few hidden, elementary principles of economics, if grasped, could give one the base to build a correct economic system. This was not a difficult task, as he made clear in his 1933 pamphlet *ABC of Economics*: the purpose of the brochure is to express the fundamentals of economics simply and clearly so that those of different schools of thought will be able to understand each other.

The Cantos, of course, interlace poetry and economics, especially from the mid 1930s on. In 1944, in fact, Pound restated the difficulty in preventing the poem from becoming pure economics: "For forty years I have schooled myself, not to write an economic history of the U.S. or any other country, but to write an epic poem which begins 'In the Dark Forest' crosses the Purgatory of human error, and ends in the light, and 'fra I maestri di color che sanno'" (*SP* 137). Ten years earlier, he understood the challenge in less allusive language:

"I have, confound it, to forge pokers, to get economic good and evil into verbal manifestation, not abstract, but so that the monetary system is as concrete as fate and *not* an abstraction etc." (*SL* 260).

To Pound, Dante and economics seemed complementary and the source of his statement "fra i maestri di color che sanno" ("I saw the master of those who know") – from Pound's Italian essay whose title is translated as "An Introduction to the Economic Nature of the United States" – is *Inferno* IV. A source of Pound's authority to make economic comments is his status as an epic poet, and to achieve this status is to discover a principle of order which is not limited to poetry. It means becoming, in a phrase Pound uses for Aristotle, "master of those that cut apart, dissect and divide" (*GK* 343).

Out of chaos comes order; out of the fragments of *The Cantos*, a kind of whole. In making the writing of his epic part of the story itself, he makes the theme of wandering, poetically and historically, his focus. This theme began and continued throughout the poem whose expansiveness is a testament to its inclusivity. This itself – the openness and ability of the poem to absorb his life as a journey – makes it a modern epic, integrating the evolving structure of the poem with his own wandering persona as he dips in and out of seemingly disconnected histories and cultures. The poetic journey becomes mythic and historical, without forgoing the personal.

Committed to the fragmented and chaotic, expressing the view that modern culture has cut loose from any tradition, Pound creates a new kind of order. The fragments appear to assemble randomly, yet an order emerges through art, implicitly ordered through aesthetics as the personal and ethical connect: "If a man have not order within him / He can not spread order about him" (XIII/59). The poet's will, in fashioning the work, establishes a perceived order, as the poet becomes a hero who makes order out of chaos and generates from a disordered reality a poetic imagining of a satisfying form. The elasticity of the wandering hero permits the movement between the shards of reality and the ideals of art.

Late in his career, Pound did not entirely lose touch with the literary world. His essays and commentaries were beginning to appear with some regularity in Italian newspapers, although often with a Fascist or economic slant. *Orientamenti* (1944) collects his Italian journalism, largely taken from *Il Meridiano di Roma* between 1938 and 1942. One item of 7 July 1940 consists of selections from *The Cantos* compiled by Olga Rudge; another is his anti-Semitic article, "L'Ebreo, patologia incarnata," of 12 October 1941. His reputation as a poet, however, was being kept alive in works like the *Oxford Book of Modern Verse* (1936), edited by Yeats, and the *Faber Book of Modern Verse* (1936), edited by Michael Roberts. Five of his poems appear in the latter work: "Near Perigord,"

"Exile's Letter," "E. P. Ode pour l'Election de son Sepulchre," "Homage to Sextus Propertius: XII," and "Canto XIII." The multiple facets of a poetic speaker who could address gaps – "a day when the historians left blanks in their writings" – deeply affected readers such as the young Scottish poet Edwin Morgan, startled by the metric freedom and new rhythms demonstrated by Pound's writing (XIII/60).

Among his prose works, *Guide to Kulchur* (1938) is perhaps Pound's fullest synthesis of political, economic and literary ideas, a combination of encyclopedia and *summa* of his thought. Money, music and cultural method are his concerns in a work that covers 2,500 years. It is a characteristic as well as fundamental Poundian text, combining overconfidence with assertiveness and directness. It is no less, he argues, than the prose equivalent of a university education, pared down, tightened and certainly advanced. With typical verve he announces that "it is my intention in this booklet to COMMIT myself on as many points as possible" (*GK* 7), and presents a work in six parts and thirteen sections, including a recapitulation (Pound is nothing if not insistent). What the table of contents does not list is that, following his "Addenda 1952," are his "Introductory Textbook" (an economics primer) and then a commentary and chronology. His music and words to "Heaulmiere" from his opera "Villon," his remarks "Villon and Comment," plus the paragraph "Condensare," end the book (*GK* 354–65).

The writing is elliptical, the tone didactic as these examples show:

> The Homeric world, very human.   (*GK* 38)

> The history of a culture is the history of ideas going into action.   (*GK* 44)

> The purpose of the writing is to reveal the subject.   (*GK* 51)

> Properly, we shd. read for power . . . the book shd. be a ball of light in one's hand.   (*GK* 55)

> The unending series of mist and mashed potatoes in the French metric didn't give the composer a chance.   (*GK* 368)

Of course, these views are not surprising coming from Pound, and from a work that concerns itself with style. Not only does the text include ideograms to reinforce the power and importance of graphic style as he discusses Confucius, but the book contains various pointers on style, which for Pound essentially means clear terms, precise definitions and the elimination of confusion.

In his abbreviated summaries of broad periods, Pound makes it clear that he abridges no extant histories, concepts or texts; in his consideration of "the New

Learning, or the New Paideuma," he is, above all, *direct*, by which he means brief (*GK* 27). By "Paideuma," borrowed from Leo Frobenius, he means "the tangle or complex of the inrooted ideas of any period," revised to mean "the gristly roots of ideas that are in action" – but definitely not the "Zeitgeist" (*GK* 57, 58). To intensify the meaning, he provides the ideogram for CH'ING MING, "the New Learning," the ideogram for mortar (*GK* 58).

Guide to Kulchur begins with a commentary on Confucius' "Digest of the Analects" which Pound balances with Pythagoras, asking the reader's indulgence: "Let the reader be patient. I am not being merely incoherent. I haven't 'lost my thread' . . . [but] I need more than one string for a fabric" (*GK* 29). Indeed, the problem as he sees it is that "whole beams and ropes of real history have been shelved, overclouded and buried" (*GK* 30). No sharp mind, he acknowledges, is ever stimulated by studying a subject "that has been put into water-tight compartments and hermetically sealed" (*GK* 32). Throughout, he pursues an "axis of reference" and follows Confucius with Athens and then Sparta in 776 BC (*GK* 34). Of particular importance is Pound's "clean cut," the distinction between ideas that exist only in a vacuum and those that are designed to go into action and serve as "rules of conduct" (*GK* 34). This repeats his directive to "cut direct" from *Gaudier-Brzeska* (*GB* 19). This difference between ideas in a vacuum and ideas in action is crucial for Pound, and the remainder of the first portion of *Guide to Kulchur* emphasizes the value of the latter.

Yet for Pound, money is never far from culture. Sparta, for example, understood it, and he provides a history of coin and the value of gold as he criticizes Athens, which was not the only center with a love of wisdom. Rome, too, possessed it. Plato, "the great-grandfather of purple patches, of prose written as cynosure for Longinus," was superseded by others, he claims (*GK* 40). Economics soon fuses with history as he reviews the pricing and taxation of Charlemagne and the ideas of Gesell and Douglas. But he is again sensitive to his reader and the possibility that his ideas are incomplete. He also recognizes that he jumps about in his cutting from the past to the present, but this method has a purpose: to compare and let readers judge and define which might be the road out of late Victorian ideological muddles. Exposure to medieval scholasticism for at least a week would order a man's ideas, he writes (*GK* 50). One must become aware – of distortions, confusions and pap.

Personal experience plays an important part in Pound's argument and he provides an amusing anecdote of working in the British Museum surrounded by volumes large and small as he calculates the way to make use of one's cultural heritage and, equally important, "corrections" (*GK* 54). Communication between scholars and the public is abysmal and standards of accuracy do not exist. Recalling the University of Pennsylvania in 1906, Pound remembers the limited view of Professor Walton Brooks McDaniel who vetoed his proposed research on Renaissance Latin because he wanted to study non-canonical authors and write a non-philological study (*GK* 215, 219). As a result, Pound moved from classical studies to Romance languages, working under Hugo Rennert on Lope de Vega. But he admits that he loathes reading: "my eyes are geared for the horizon. Nevertheless I do read for days on end when I have caught the scent of a trail" (*GK* 55).

Historiography becomes an important feature of *Guide to Kulchur*. Relations, not dates or details matter, while audience is essential, Pound explaining that it is not what a man says that is valuable but what part of it his auditors consider important. We do not, he writes, know the past chronologically, even though it may be convenient to "lay it out anesthetized on the table with dates pasted on here and there"; "what we know we know by ripples and spirals eddying out from us and from our own time" (*GK* 59–60). This asymmetric concept of history is precisely what Pound represents in *The Cantos* with its varying emphases and jumps. The best history you can write, he implies, is by "tracing ideas, exposing the growth of a concept" (*GK* 60). This is Pound's method.

Section II of the first part, Pound calls "Vortex," and it restates ideas he earlier presented as Vorticism, beginning with comments on Gaudier-Brzeska written by John Cournos and continuing with a note from Gaudier-Brzeska written from the trenches. "Great Bass: Part One" opens the next section and it is the first of two parts focusing on semi-technical features of music but with philosophy as a backdrop, ranging from Spinoza to Leibniz. Pound adds here that "*these disjunct paragraphs belong together . . .* [and] *are parts of one ideogram*," not merely separate subjects (*GK* 75). In a following section, "Tradition," he pits the Greeks and the Church against Confucius; the West loses. The Confucian "Great Learning [is] the examination of a motivation," he emphasizes, "an examination with a clear purpose" (*GK* 79). Here, he expresses his method again, claiming that the Confucian Great Learning "is a root, the centre of steadily out-circling causations from immediate order to a whole series of harmonies and good conducts" (*GK* 79–80; cf. 83).

Part II begins with a focus on artists, notably Picabia and Duchamp, but leads to an indictment of French avant-garde culture. Italy comes next, praised and upheld as the sensational center of culture. Aeschylus and the history of philosophy follow, although occasionally the titles mislead: "Monumental" deals not with sculpture or architecture but with Joyce (*GK* 96). "Values," the opening of Part III, deals with genius and the importance of "volcanic and disordered" minds like that of Wyndham Lewis (*GK* 106). Pound then proceeds to address Dante on the troubadours in one of his longest sections, "Europe or The Setting," a broadly based overview of European writing and culture with examples of "Paideuma," where memory plays a crucial role (*GK* 108–9). "For 31 years," he writes, "I have carried in my mind as a species of rich diagram, the Prado as I saw it . . ." (*GK* 110). But he quickly switches to 1938 and how it would be possible to get "the best of Europe." Is a walking tour still possible? he asks. Food becomes a new fascination, declaring that "Le Voyage Gastronomique is a French paideuma. Outside it, you can get English roast beef in Italy (if you spend 25 years learning how) . . ." (*GK* 112). His catalogue of culture continues, blended with economics, politics and his own personal progress.

Literature, however, becomes an equal force, presented in the language and terms of politics. Poetry, he announces at one point, "is totalitarian in any confrontation with prose. There is MORE in and on two pages of poetry than in or on ten pages of any prose save the few books that rise above classification as anything save exceptions" (*GK* 121). It is evident that, for Pound at this time (1938), the literary cannot be divorced from the political and his definition of "Kulchur" takes on a coloration defined by social needs and economic realities.

At the center of Pound's world is Kung (Confucius) whose ethics travel up and down the cultural ladder, from philosophy to literature, from business to individual relationships. And from his own perspective, Pound unleashes his own criticism: Plato is a "purple swine" for advocating the expulsion of poets' Puccini "knows how to write for the bawlers. I mean he KNOWS how"; "The Bourbons were garbage. The French court was punk" (*GK* 128, 155, 230). But in so doing, he echoes his own practice, declaring that "an imperfect broken statement if uttered in sincerity often tells more to the auditor than the most meticulous caution of utterance could" (*GK* 129). The remark is a concentrated reader's guide to *The Cantos*, expanded when he cites the works of Boccherini and Bartók, which, like his *Cantos*, are a "record of a personal struggle" with the "defects inherent in a record of struggle" (*GK* 135). In an aside to his publishers, he declares that if they expect a linear, chronological presentation of culture, they will not find it "HERE" (*GK* 129).

Pound gradually approaches a definition of culture, although negatively: "Knowledge is NOT culture. The domain of culture begins when one HAS 'forgotten-what-book,'" implying self-discovery and self-awareness as the key (*GK* 134). The encyclopedic and ahistorical structure continues throughout the final chapters of *Guide to Kulchur*, although one chapter title is a date – "March 12th" – in which, as he outlines the nature of poetry, he tells his reader this is where one should pause for reflection (*GK* 138). Yet Pound loves to conflate, as a single sentence at the end of Chapter 24 illustrates, uniting Dante, a race driver and Thomas Edison (*GK* 161).

No subject seems beyond Pound in this work: textbooks, Italian schools, Renaissance writing styles, musical structures, the *Odyssey* (which, with the *Ta Hio*, he someday hopes to read without the need of dictionaries), Martin Van Buren's autobiography, university education, Aristotle and ideograms all come under review (*GK* 144ff.). In the process, he also moves closer to defining a culture, which for him means learning to act on one's definitions and to discover what an individual or an age "really wishes to *do*" (*GK* 144).

As he proceeds, Pound unites Confucius and Mussolini because they both recognize that "their people need poetry" and realize that "prose is NOT education but the outer courts of the same" (*GK* 144). Only by great labor can one gain the inner sanctum of cultural and personal self-knowledge. What Pound drives at is a "new learning," placing new importance on what he calls "the *forma*," the immortal concept or "dynamic form which is like the rose pattern driven into the dead iron-filings by the magnet, not by material contact with the magnet itself, but separate from the magnet. Cut off by the layer of glass, the dust and filings rise and spring into order. Thus, the *forma*, the concept rises from death" (*GK* 152).

While he orchestrates ideas of culture from varying historical periods, Pound criticizes himself for becoming too general, getting too far from concrete and particular objects (*GK* 166). He also restates his view that we err if we believe that our system of categories is the only possible kind. Yet any art that leads to "more exact definition[s] is positive," and that which is expressed by a cut, definite and exact, is valuable. The verb is important and links Gaudier-Brzeska ("cut direct") with music: "The performing musician cuts his form in the air and in the time flow" (*GK* 169, 170). In *How to Read*, he wrote that "rhythm is a form cut into TIME" (*ABCR* 198). For Pound, this is an art because a cut is clear and undisputed, as Dante, the "master of those that cut apart, dissect and divide," demonstrated in the language of *The Divine Comedy* (*GK* 343).

As he moves toward a conclusion, Pound becomes ironically self-conscious of his project, prepared to criticize his own work. The first paragraph of Chapter 29, "Guide to Kulchur," opens with: "Ridiculous title, stunt piece. Challenge? Guide, ought to mean help other fellow to get there. Ought one turn up one's nose? Trial shots. 18th century *in the main*, cliché. 19th mainly MESS" (*GK* 183). He then addresses eighteenth-century poetry, especially Samuel Johnson's "Vanity of Human Wishes," and explains that any understanding of a civilization means the "comprehension of incompatibles" (*GK* 184). But for Pound, the true test of ideas is when "they go into action," which he believes his *Cantos* demonstrate, implicitly parallel to Dante's *Divine Comedy* (*GK* 188,

194). They, *The Cantos*, are not mysterious: "they are the tale of the tribe" (borrowing a phrase from Kipling) (*GK* 194). And as he proceeds, he simplifies, or, rather, finds aphoristic statements to express complex ideas: "History that omits economics is mere bunk" (*GK* 259). Pound understands that directness is essential to clarity, and his pithy statements outline a methodology of research as well as study. He also pointedly notes that the results of research without "some concept to work to" are exceptionally dull: "Not the document but the significance of the document" matters, adding that that was where nineteenth-century philology went astray – which he himself tried to revise in his study of Cavalcanti. "Some kind of line to hang one's facts on is better than no line at all," he re-emphasizes (*GK* 221).

Yet fact and its interpretation are not enough in *Guide to Kulchur*. Pound also has room for "the celestial tradition," the world of ideal forms Plato initiated. Pound tries to balance "man inebriated with infinity, on the one hand, and man with a millimetric measure and microscope on the other" (*GK* 222–3). The first step is the definition of terms. In this section, where Pound documents the ideas of Gemistus Plethon who brought a form of Platonism to Italy in the fifteenth-century, he comes alive, writing forcefully and with new energy as he struggles to balance objectivism and ecstasy (*GK* 224–5). He also knows that "inner harmony seldom leads to active perturbing of public affairs"; the well-balanced do not disrupt the social order (*GK* 225). Government, economics (he now criticizes Douglas for not accepting Gesell's views) and the nature of money now overtake his writing, but, throughout his analysis, the Poundian method is always at work: "first the clear definition, then the clear articulation" (*GK* 248).

A new undercurrent soon emerges. Strands of anti-Semitism appear in the work, from his early suggestion that "the forbidden fruit of Hebrew story is a usury parable," to an implicit praise of Wyndham Lewis' discovery of Hitler, superior to his own discovery of Mussolini and Jews who "slither on" with talk about "influences" (*GK* 42, 134, 236). Pound complicates the matter with passages that also compliment Jews, noting that, his own "predisposition being nomadic, "it is" not for me to rebuke brother semite for similar disposition" (*GK* 243). He also criticizes the English for reviling the Jews for beating them at their own game (*GK* 243). Pound's energy is unaffected as he ambitiously declares, near the end of his book, that if his anthology *Des Imagistes* initiated the renovation of poetry, he was now ready to "delouse the presentation of 17th and 18th (and 15th for that matter) century music or even a little contemporary composition, by analogous process, at least under favourable or exceptional conditions (say in the town hall of Rapallo, if powerless to affect the more bulbous fatty and opulent festivals)" (*GK* 253).

If Pound's energy has so far not been convincing, he closes with a recapitulation in which, with an ideogram to power the section, he reiterates the force of Confucius, the importance of clarity, the role of Plato and Aristotle, and a review of his topics with page numbers, forming a mini table of contents (*GK* 348). Six points summarize his position, while a "Sextant," a kind of postscript listing a revised core reading list, concludes the *Guide*. Following, however, is his *Introductory Text Book*. Pound could not stop teaching, nor condensing. Appropriately, the final section of the *Guide to Kulchur* is headed "Condensare."

Pound was a polarizing figure, no more so than when he addressed anti-Semitism and racism in his writing and radio broadcasts. Variously excused as suburban prejudice, something he grew up with in Philadelphia, or a minor excess contradicted by his friendships with individual Jews like Louis Zukofsky, it remained offensive. Basil Bunting, James Laughlin, William Carlos Williams and Marianne Moore all objected. "It makes me sick to see you covering yourself with that filth," Bunting told Pound, while Laughlin declared, "I think anti-Semitism is contemptible and despicable and I will not put my hand to it."[15] Many could not understand Pound's virulent, irrational attacks, although at the very end of his life he tried to explain it as a distortion. Yet his iteration of anti-Semitism persists as an obstacle to his popularity and acceptance, fulfilling a line from his early poem, "Und Drang": "the deed blots out the thought" (*EPEW* 28).

Anti-Semitic lines appear throughout the poetry, at one point forcing Laughlin to black out text in Canto LII when it appeared in the US. The text was restored only in the tenth printing of *The Cantos* in 1986 (LII/257–8). In the first thirty cantos, no anti-Semitic remarks exist, although Pound quotes a Mustafa, who, in response to Pound's remark that his Jewish guide to Gibraltar, Yusuf, is a good fellow, responds with "But after all a chew / ees a chew" (XX/105). Three anti-Semitic passages, however, appear in *The Pisan Cantos*, as well as in his late "Addendum" for Canto C, a sermon against usury. But early work also reflected his antagonistic view, "Salutation the Third" being but one example: "Let us be done with Jews and Jobbery," he writes, "Let us SPIT upon those who fawn on the JEWS for their money" (*EPPT* 1312).[16]

The Rome radio broadcasts, made from January 1941 to July 1943 (when Mussolini's government fell), contain the most offensive passages. In one or two sentences he would conflate attacks on Jews, America and Roosevelt, declaring on 14 March 1943, for example, that "The USA will be no use to itself or to anyone else until it gets rid of the kikes AND Mr. Roosevelt" (*EPS* 246). That he made these broadcasts against the background of the Holocaust only adds to the furore against him. "Should Ezra Pound be Shot?" was the title of a 25 December 1945 article in the *New Masses*, four days after he was transferred from Gallinger Hospital to St. Elizabeths Federal Hospital for the Insane in Washington and placed in solitary confinement. In the radio broadcasts, stereotypes abound, from Jews controlling the banks and finances of America and Europe to their unwillingness to mix or assimilate with others.

After 1935, Pound's manic tendencies – frantic letter writing, grandiose economic objectives – became more pronounced and his broadcasts reflected a kind of manic speech: loud, rapid, intense, jokey, theatrical and hostile. He believed in a Jewish master plan and control: "The Jews have ruin'd every country they have got hold of" and they have worked out a system "for the ruin of the rest of mankind, one nation after another," he declared on 21 March 1943 (*EPS* 256). The Jews and Jewish texts were also responsible for Communism: "The Talmud is the one and only begetter of the Bolshevik system," according to Pound who also believed that Jews controlled the press as well as international banking (*EPS* 117).

Can one defend Pound's anti-Semitism? Of course not. Can one explain it? Not entirely. Some have tried to understand it in terms of his psychotic deterioration, others as a deep-seated but complex hatred of the "other." Some readers /critics try to avoid it entirely, concentrating on aesthetic issues and finding New Criticism a useful excuse for addressing only Pound's work, not his ideas. Others, however, denounced him – Pound in a sense denouncing himself when he told Allen Ginsberg in 1967 that his writing was "stupidity and ignorance all the way through" and that his "worst mistake" was his "stupid, suburban prejudice of anti-Semitism [which] all along . . . spoiled everything."[17]

Denunciations of modernism as Fascism in literary form, offered in sweeping post-structuralist statements, are too simple. Yet the bankruptcy of modernism, occurring because of a crisis in the critical interpretation of politics and poetry, has some critics seeking an alternative term, possibly "avant-garde." Pound's explicit Fascist statements and anti-Semitic invective, complemented by Eliot's authoritarianism and his poetry's anti-Semitic allusions, plus Yeats' pro-Fascist leanings and Lewis' support of Hitler, compromise and complicate the concept of modernism. Pound's anti-Semitism remains a difficult aspect of his career that has impinged on the broad acceptance of his work – as it has raised questions about the work of Eliot and Yeats – at the same time that it prolongs the debate about whether or not one should dismiss modernist writing on the grounds of reprehensible attitudes.[18] Pound's psychotic state of mind may have played a part in his anti-Semitism but the difficulties it has presented have not entirely been erased by his poetic excellence or critical acumen.

In the post-Second World War period, Pound also published a series of notable translations, including *The Unwobbling Pivot & The Great Digest* by Confucius and *The Women of Trachis* by Sophocles. He also worked on such anthologies as *The Classic Anthology Defined by Confucius* and *Confucius to Cummings* – and wrote voluminous letters to newspapers, journals, congressmen, poets, novelists and friends. Pound was also, and continuously, a moralist. He wanted to show that literature mattered, that it had a crucial role in keeping the language clean, society stable. He made this clear in the *ABC of Reading* in which he emphasized that literature "does not exist in a vacuum. Writers as such have a definite social function exactly proportioned to their ability AS WRITERS." This, he adds, "is their main use." Furthermore, if a "nation's literature declines, the nation atrophies and decays" (*ABCR* 32). The very role of the poet is to see that this does not happen, as he explained to Basil Bunting in a letter of 1935 in which he identified great art as the union of surface with justice (*SL* 277). It is that last word that matters, bringing a Confucian sense of socio-political order to art.

Pound seemed to have little creative energy left over for writing more poetry in the 1950s, although he felt an urgency to finish *The Cantos*. But by the 1960s, he felt he had botched it: "any good has been spoiled by my intentions – the preoccupation with irrelevant and stupid things," he told Allen Ginsberg (Ginsberg 4–5). In a curious way, this echoes Count Ugolino in the *Divine Comedy* who, also in a Pisa prison, tells Dante: "if my words are seed from which the fruit is infamy . . . you'll see me speak and weep at once."[19] But, like its very theme and representation of the unstructured (and the possible beauty that might emerge from it), *The Cantos* – appropriately – ends unfinished, becoming the very thing it was about. To complete the work would be to undo it.

But Pound was also beginning to recognize his limitations: "Damn it all, I am a poek, partly a musician, i.e., in one corner up to a point, and a economist. I can't become an authority on another dept. in six weeks or even six months. Time is past for me to do interim stuff, and ex cathedra? NO" (*SL* 341). Here, he lists his identities: poet, musician, economist. By the forties, when he wrote this paragraph, and after, the three roles were intersecting in ways even Pound had not anticipated.

The importance of *The Cantos* and Pound's poetry can be measured in numerous ways. One of the most important is their demonstration that art can be made from pieces, something Gertrude Stein, Picasso and Joyce confirmed. The sense of order and coherence Victorian and earlier literature required was no longer viable in an age that had itself fallen apart because of war, economics and history. Pound showed, furthermore, that poetry can be a process of thinking rather than a report of things already thought. Additionally, Pound's avoidance of a national or geographically centered poetry set the course for a new universal modernism, based in part on a recovery of the Provençal as much as of the Orient. Pound's principle of juxtaposition, of inter-cutting, of cultural overlaying, with ideas or ideograms butting against one another, constructed a transatlantic modernism which influenced a generation of later writers. *The Cantos* stands not so much as an obstacle but a mountain which very few can avoid. It is a field of action that requires crossing.

Chapter 4

Critical reception

Yeats used to say I was trying to provide a portable substitute for the British Museum.

Ezra Pound, 1934

Readers, critics and the public did not know what to make of Pound. His politics were extreme, his criticism abrasive and his poetry complex. Unlike T. S. Eliot or Joyce, he never had a "bestseller" – a work of popular appeal or commercial success. *The Waste Land* and *Ulysses* were internationally recognized. Pound never had a poem so widely accepted, although his presence was indisputable, as Carl Sandburg explained: "All talk on modern poetry, by people who know, ends with dragging in Ezra Pound somewhere. He may be named only to be cursed as wanton and mocker, poseur, trifler and vagrant. Or he may be classed as filling a niche today like that of Keats in a preceding epoch. The point is, he will be mentioned" (*CRH* 112).

The only text of Pound's that seemed to obtain wide recognition was his two line, haiku-like, "In a Station of the Metro." When he did receive attention, it was more for controversy rather than praise. The Bollingen Prize of 1949, for example, led to tremendous battles in the press and in the US Congress over awarding a prize from the Library of Congress to a traitor and anti-Semite. When he returned to Italy following his release in 1958, his photograph stirred new resentments: with arm raised, he gave the Fascist salute and told reporters that "All America is an insane asylum" (SCh 848). When a committee nominated him for the Emerson–Thoreau Medal of the American Academy of Arts and Sciences in 1972, the executive council turned him down. The controversy continued for two months but the decision was unchanged. Even in old age, his notoriety was undiminished, his readership select, his influence great.

As an editor, critic and promoter of writers, Pound had his supporters and they were unwavering. Ernest Hemingway wrote in *A Moveable Feast* that "Ezra Pound was the most generous writer I have ever known and the most disinterested. He helped poets, painters, sculptors and prose writers that he believed in and he would help anyone whether he believed in them or not if they were in trouble." Yeats recalled that "he has great influence, more perhaps than any contemporary except Eliot." Joyce told Yeats that Pound was a "miracle worker" for getting *Portrait* in print, and e. e. cummings referred to Pound as "the true trailblazer of an epoch." T. S. Eliot offered one of the most important encomiums when he dedicated *The Waste Land* to Pound, using Dante's words from *Purgatorio*, Canto 26, where Dante praises Arnaut Daniel as *il miglior fabbro*, "the better craftsman."[1]

Pound's obsessive economic ideas and repellant anti-Semitism, however, overshadowed his poetry. But when it *was* discussed, terms like "obscure" "knotty" or "difficult" were used. His opinionated and absolute literary criticism has similarly been questioned, although, more recently, Pound's poetic practice, separated from his economic and political ideas, has received greater attention. Anthologies, however, continue to under-represent his work, limiting examples to selected early works, largely Imagist or from *Cathay*. Occasionally, a section from *Mauberley*, buttressed with excerpts from the Malatesta or *Pisan Cantos*, appears. The new *Oxford Book of American Poetry* (2006), edited by David Lehman, is representative. Eliot, Williams and Wallace Stevens have larger contributions, with John Ashbery represented by twice as many pages as Pound. The latter's restless, iconoclastic, ambitious, unrestrained and flawed writing has not achieved wide acceptance.

The hesitant reception of Pound's work began during his lifetime, T. S. Eliot anonymously publishing a 31-page pamphlet entitled *Ezra Pound, His Metric and Poetry* (1917) in an effort to explain Pound's writing. Through a careful discussion of his poetic progress, Eliot personalizes Pound's work, offering details of composition and method to make the poetry more accessible and understandable, often including useful reviews. More importantly, Eliot identifies the technical elements of the poetry, noting that Pound's ability to adapt meter to mood, possible only after intensive study, is as remarkable as his restraint in using *vers libre*. Additionally, no word of Pound's is thoughtlessly chosen, and in his experiments with form, whether the ballads of Cavalcanti or "The Seafarer," Pound succeeds. Pound does make demands on the reader, but they are always rewarded. Eliot ends with comment on the first three Cantos.

The catalyst for Eliot's pamphlet was critical resistance to Pound's early poetry, which ranged from derision to parody. *Punch* satirized it and Ford Madox Ford took his famous roll on a Giessen floor as Pound read him passages from *Canzoni*. A readership formed by Yeats, Harriet Monroe, Ford, Joyce and Eliot was not enough to overcome critical rejection. *Personae* (1909) was thought affectatious and occasionally incoherent, although sincere by a poet with a distinct personality working with forms other poets might study

(*CRH* 46–7). Rupert Brooke, a star among Edwardian poets, reluctantly praised Pound – "when he has passed through stammering to speech . . . he may be a great poet" – although he later repented this prediction (*CRH* 59).

Exultations met with a reception usually reserved for a scholarly work containing French, Provençal, Spanish, Italian, Latin and Old English works. "Piere Vidal Old" and "Ballad of the Goodly Fere" were singled out for praise. *Canzoni* (1911) met with strong opposition, however, one critic declaring it "ought never to have been printed," citing its "eccentric forms or eccentric no-forms," supported by careless rhythms (*CRH* 78–9). The major problem was "the jargon and jingle of his titles and of some of his lines [which] suggest his desire to write in a dozen languages at once" (*CRH* 79). Affectation combined with pedantry was the conclusion of the *Westminster Gazette*, while the *Poetry Review* suggested that, if Pound could translate a poem, he would do so rather than make one. Indeed, the review continues, even his own poems read as if they were translations (*CRH* 85).

Ripostes (1912), Pound's fourth book, met with equally mixed reviews. "We do not understand its aims," said *The Times Literary Supplement*, although *Poetry and Drama* found technical achievements in a summary essay by F. S. Flint where he praised *Canzoni* as a "masterpiece of quiet, patient irony" (*CRH* 96). The sapphics of "Apparuit," the rhythm of "The Return" and the alliterative verse of "The Seafarer" all earn praise. *Cathay* (1915) was Pound's first work to earn general approval, creating, as Ford writes, "a landscape made real by the intensity of human emotions" (*CRH* 109). The reprint of "The Seafarer" in the volume again earned praise.

In 1916, Carl Sandburg expressed admiration for Pound as the one individual who had done most "to incite new impulses in poetry" (*CRH* 112). But *Lustra*, criticized for its detachment and satire, found little sympathy because it was too bookish and retreated from life into literature. All Pound did was collect cultures which gave him no more than "an accent, an attitude," a critic complained. Pound had little to say but said it in a way that gave his words "superficial significance" (*CRH* 130–1). The gesture, not the phrase, distinguishes his work which is no more than "poetry in pantomime" (*CRH* 131).

Pound's prose fared no better, *Pavannes and Divisions* described as "malformed models, filings and tailings from the craftsman's workshop" (*CRH* 143). Pound had been diverted and put his "trivialities, translations [and] annotated excerpts" into type. His creative talent had gone sterile, making a "disorderly retreat into the mazes of technique and pedantry" (*CRH* 142). His inability to command attention and dissatisfaction with his age were thought to be the cause of his "splenetic outbursts" (*CRH* 144). Such truculence, however, was tiresome. The reckless poet of 1910 becomes no more than a "sophisticated *proseur*" who "declined into querulous dogmatizing." But, as a "publicist, he has few equals" (*CRH* 144, 145).

"Homage to Sextus Propertius" intensified criticism of Pound, the Professor of Latin at the University of Chicago, W. G. Hale, castigating him for the "undignified" and "flippant" manner of his translation, things which Propertius never was (*CRH* 155). The version actually dragged because Pound had padded the text, a text harmed by numerous errors of translation. Blunders appeared everywhere and "If Mr. Pound were a professor of Latin, there would be nothing left for him but suicide" (*CRH* 157). Eliminate the mask of erudition, advised the professor. *Quia Pauper Amavi* (1919), which reprinted "Propertius," met with reserved negativism including early criticism of "Three Cantos" ("going Browning's *Sordello* one better"): after some "acute criticism, [it] skips through the continents and the centuries, whisking us from Egypt to Provence and then to Spain (*via* Japan) in a few pages" (*CRH* 160). English reviewers were more sympathetic toward Pound's jaunty and modern Propertius, which was not, he was at pains to point out, a translation.

The *Observer*, however, was less forgiving, complaining that *Quia Pauper Amavi* varies from his best to his worst, the Provençal forms showing his impudence, pedantry and yet true regard for poetry. "Langue d'Oc" received high praise but the second section of "*Moeurs Contemporaines*" was called only "poor prose cut into lengths. It is not poetry, though it pretends to the satire" (*CRH* 165). "Three Cantos" was merely an "ingenious essay" trying to say "a possible something of your own in the words of another." Pound confused "the profound and the obscure" (*CRH* 166). Reading the poem was more like taking a minor literary examination. It was a "ragbag without synthesis," since Pound had "smothered the *thing itself* in the tatters of second-hand clothes" (*CRH* 166). Pound seemed determined to "wear his perverse, ironical, intellectually snobbish panache at all costs" (*CRH* 166).

Pound's personality seemed to many readers to dominate his poetry – a personality described as: a "queer compost of harsh levity, spite, cocksureness, innuendo, pedantry, archaism, sensuality, real if sometimes perverse and unfortunate research and honest love of literature. In the end, of course, tedium supervenes, since nothing is more tiring than a tireless *scherzo*. But the work is amusing. Let Mr. Pound stick to the mask" (CRH 167). Gradually, a counter-swell supportive of Pound's work emerged. John Gould Fletcher in 1920 claimed that the poetry, *not* the personality of Pound, should be the focus. Beauty, not satire, was Pound's aim, he stated, "a beauty hard, bright, tangible, vividly American in its abrupt quality of definition, if not in its *mise-en-scène*" (*CRH* 172). Here, Pound's action and energy and definiteness are explained as American.

It was *Exultations* that revealed most clearly Pound's mastery in producing poetry no Englishman could write – the *vers libre* experiments of *Ripostes* and *Cathay*, the free, broken blank verse of 'Near Perigord' and "Three Cantos," additional examples of his originality. But these works, while fascinating to study, were not poetry because they did not engage the reader, Fletcher claimed. May Sinclair in the *North American Review* of May 1920, however, furthered support for Pound in a lengthy essay declaring he was anything but a "literary mountebank" and that what he did for Gaudier-Brzeska, Joyce, Lewis and Eliot was extra-ordinary (*CRH* 178). Pound was an original, she argued, with a genius for literary impersonation. But all approaches to this poet were "difficult. Unless you love sudden, strange, disconcerting beauty and certain qualities that he has brought into literature, of bright hardness, of harshness, of intellectual flame" (*CRH* 181).

The publication of *Hugh Selwyn Mauberley* in 1920 did not advance Pound's reputation. Many found it cryptic and obscure, the many diverse sections confirming the fragmented and disjointed character of Pound's writing. *The Times Literary Supplement* referred to it as an "esoteric volume" appealing only to a small readership, despite the author's obsession with "the greater semi-artistic public" (*CRH* 194). Edwin Muir in the *New Age* objected to the acerbity of the poem and its replacement of satire with despair. Readers also rejected Pound's critique, complaining that he was "an incomparable *causeur*" (*CRH* 189).

Pound's work up to 1925, when *A Draft of XVI Cantos* appeared, met with constant opposition if not hostility, a situation compounded by his perceived egoism, "*subfusc* pedantry" and Americanness (*CRH* 173). The support of Yeats, Ford and Lewis did little to expand his readership. Pound remained an outsider, never "at home in twentieth century Europe" according to Fletcher. He could only get life out of books and was unable to convey the emotions or intimacy of individuals in his poetry (*CRH* 173). His "opaque isolation" fascinated less than it distanced. But in America, H. L. Mencken saw this as a plus. While recognizing Pound's "pertinacious bellicosity, his abysmal learning, his delight in the curious," he nonetheless calls him the "most extraordinary man that American literature has seen in our time" but one who characteristically "keeps as far away from America as possible" (*CRH* 190). Harold Monro, poet and editor of the *Poetry Review*, summed up the response to the first half of Pound's career when he remarked that "the recognition of his genius will be gradual and tardy" (*CRH* 175).

The publication of *The Cantos* in volumes spread out over a 44-year period increased the difficulty of accessing and understanding the work. The appearance of individual, or sets of, Cantos in "brave magazines" was like "a block of cumbersome, streaked marble . . . as if on a pedestal of temporary stucco and obscured by scaffolding," wrote the American critic Glenway Wescott (*CRH* 215). When individual volumes did appear, they were often in expensive deluxe editions which made their accessibility more restricted. And readers still remained lost, viewing the texts as only "the nervous attempt of a poet to probe and mould the residue left by the books and tales that he has absorbed" (*CRH* 206). Publishers recognized this. When the trade edition of *A Draft of XXX Cantos* appeared in New York in 1933, it included a 22-page pamphlet entitled *The Cantos of Ezra Pound, Some Testimonies*, with statements on the importance of the poem by Hemingway, Ford Madox Ford, Eliot, Joyce, H. D. and Basil Bunting. New Directions, sensing objections to the poem's obscurity, felt the need for the publication. The publisher duplicated the process with another pamphlet accompanying their edition of *Cantos LII–LXXI* (1940), containing an essay by James Laughlin (signed H. H.) and one by the poet Delmore Schwartz (signed S.D.).

Yeats did not help. In his "Preface" to the *Oxford Book of Modern Verse* (1936), he criticized the disruptive text of *The Cantos*, complaining that while it had more style than any other contemporary poem that he knew, it was also "constantly interrupted, broken, twisted into nothing by its direct opposite, nervous obsession, nightmare, stammering confusion . . . style and its opposite can alternate, but form must be full, sphere-like, single." There are also "unbridged transitions, unexplained ejaculations, that make his meaning unintelligible." Other critics of the thirties, such as Geoffrey Grigson, were similarly displeased by the apparent lack of structure and organic form, although, early on, William Carlos Williams understood the structural principle at work. He identified this as the major move in imaginative writing of the time: a shift away from the word as symbol to the word as reality. Montage replaced symbolism.[2]

When *The Cantos* began to appear in a single volume in 1948, they were still incomplete, since Pound continued to add material up to 1969. It wasn't until the thirteenth printing in 1995 that the so-called "Italian Cantos" (Cantos LXXII and LXXIII) were placed in their proper order and that the work could in any fashion be called "finished." That term is itself questionable, however, since the final section of the poem, printed largely for copyright reasons, is called only *Drafts & Fragments* (1969). 'Fragment (1966)," in praise of Olga Rudge, is the concluding section. But dispute still exists over what *is* the proper ending.

Pound, himself, had difficulty evaluating his work, often drawing on musical analogies, first the fugue and then Bartók's *Fifth Quartet* which he cites in *Guide to Kulchur* (*GK* 135). In a series of letters beginning in 1927, he remarks that the structure of the work is "rather like, or unlike, subject and response and counter subject in fugue" (*SL* 210). Yeats took this up as an adequate explanation in

A Vision, writing that when Pound comes to his hundredth canto it would "display a structure like that of a Bach fugue. There will be no plot . . . but two themes, the Descent into Hades from Homer, a Metamorphosis from Ovid." Mixed in would be medieval or modern historical characters (*AV* 3–5).

Pound found the Yeats passage irksome and too simple, although in 1937 he hesitatingly repeated the fugue analogy: "Take a fugue: theme, response, contrasujet. *Not* that I mean to make an exact analogy of structure" (*P/J* 35; *SL* 294). In *Guide to Kulchur*, however, he offers another musical example, citing again Bartók's *Fifth Quartet* which "is the record of a personal struggle, possible only to a man born in the 1880s. It has the defects or disadvantages of my Cantos" (*GK* 134). Pound had heard the piece at a Rapallo concert, the abrasive harmonies and irregular rhythms similar, he thought, to the structure and movement of his own poem. But he apparently heard the Bartók only once and did not notice its formal, if unusual, symmetry.

Critics reacted to individual volumes of *The Cantos* with hesitancy or confusion. Louis Zukofsky, an early Pound disciple and subsequent leader of the Objectivist movement – he had attended the Ezuversity in 1933 in Rapallo – wrote an early appreciation. His 1929 essay emphasized the moral and restorative power of Pound's language, noting that words are for him, "principles of a line of action."[3] Zukofsky underscores Pound's application of the Ta Hio or Great Learning as a gauge of action for life in the present. Pound, he writes, has been "both the isolated creator and the worldly pamphleteer" (Zukofsky 63). His translation also received praise, with emphasis on Pound's "distinction of rendering into English unexplored poetic forms and of translating himself through personae" (Zukofsky 65). In commenting on Cantos I–XXVII, Zukofsky praises their "world of oneness, notwithstanding a multiplicity of speech" (Zukofsky 67).

Zukofsky sees Pound's work as one of tension between the narrator and those who obstruct knowledge and distribution, as in Cantos XIV and XVI. Zukofsky recognizes, however, that *The Cantos* are unique in Pound's work and could not be fully understood through the forms of the shorter poems, although he does state that "Imagism and music direct the composition" of the poem, referring to its energy as "imagism-in-music" (Zukofsky 75). Pound's parsimonious use of adjectives, however, contributes to the sheerness of the language and imagery as he makes his subject-matter his style.

Zukofsky believed that Pound's prose contains the best explication of *The Cantos* and he lists prose parallels for individual Cantos, noting that, to understand Pound's use of Andreas Divus's version of *The Odyssey*, one should read Pound's "Translators of the Greek" from *Instigations*. Zukofsky also identifies the links showing how the ideation of Dante's *Divine Comedy* refers to

Virgil who referred to Homer who is, of course, used, via a Latin translation, by Pound. Zukofsky insightfully shows that Dante's *Inferno, Purgatorio* and *Paradiso* become, in Pound's world, hate, comprehension and worship, not "religious geometry," intersecting or juxtaposed to one another (Zukofsky 69).

What appealed most to Zukofsky is the immediacy of Pound's epic matter – which he identifies as the form of *The Cantos* – making sudden shifts from Odysseus to Sordello or from Proteus to the Dorgan's steps, which Zukofsky calls the "complete passage through, in and around objects, historical events, the living them at once." This is as much a fact as those facts historians label and disassociate (Zukofsky 71). The music via meter in the poem is also suggestive to Zukofsky who approvingly quotes Pound's declaration in *Pavannes & Divagations* that "progress lies rather in an attempt to approximate classical quantitative meters (NOT to copy them) than in a careless regarding such things." The appeal of *The Cantos* to Zukofsky is musical, as he cites lines from Canto XXVII:

> And the waves like a forest
> Where the wind is weightless in the leaves
> But moving,
>   so that the sound runs upon sound.
>   (XXVII/131)

In 1931, Zukofsky published three other essay-reviews of Pound's work in *Criterion, Front* and *Poetry.* Not surprisingly, Zukofsky would inherit a Poundian sense of poetic experience as the key to understanding poetic expression. In reading a poem, he wrote in 1950, one "becomes something of a poet himself: not because he 'contributes' to the poetry, but because he finds himself subject of its energy" (Zukofsky 31). Zukofsky would also publish his own semi-Poundian set of translations of Catullus.

Basil Bunting also wrote about *The Cantos,* although in less detail but with enthusiasm equal to Zukofsky's. Bunting's "Mr. Ezra Pound" appeared in the *New English Weekly* for 26 May 1932, just as attention to Pound's work was increasing, prompted by the appearance of *A Draft of XXX Cantos* (1930). William Carlos Williams jotted down his impressions of the first thirty Cantos, praising the exactness of the imagery: "It stands out from almost all other verse by a faceted quality that is not muzzy, painty, wet. It is a dry, clean use of words."[4]

Reviews, however, were extreme, either praising or damning the work, one writer in 1933 complaining of the poet's use of contemporary references and lack of structure and continuity.[5] Two years earlier, however, Marianne Moore wrote an enthusiastic review, praising Pound's technique. But she also raised an ethical question: why can't "money and life go for beauty instead of war and intellectual oppression?" In a 1934 review, she praises the metrical effects declaring that there is "a wisdom as remarkable as anything since Bach."[6] The musical analogy would have no doubt pleased Pound who was, nonetheless, becoming defensive, asking critics to wait until all the cantos were published before offering comments on the form of the whole (*SL* 323).

Yeats continued to defend Pound's work, although with some skepticism. Expanding his introduction to the *Oxford Book of Modern Verse*, Yeats writes that Pound's theme is flux, but notes that characterization, plot and local discourse "seem to him abstractions unsuitable to a man of his generation." He does hope, however, that the relation of the elements to each other will be apparent when "the whole is finished." But "like other readers, I discover at present merely exquisite or grotesque fragments," he honestly reports (in Sullivan 183). Pound's belief in his own conception had been so great, he adds, that since the appearance of Canto I, he (Yeats) had tried to suspend judgment. Another poet, Yvor Winters, also tried to decipher the structure of *The Cantos*, writing in 1937 that Pound proceeded from image to image and that his only principle was mood, varied and established. Each statement is reasonable in itself but the progression from statement to statement is not. Yet the work is "the most ambitious attempt of our century to create a carry-all form" (in Sullivan 186, 188).

Critics between 1930 and 1950, however, were not making much headway with the text. Pound's work remained opaque, enigmatic and apparently impregnable. Then Hugh Kenner published *The Poetry of Ezra Pound* in 1951 with this challenging opening: "There is no great contemporary writer who is less read than Ezra Pound" (*PEP* 16). He then carefully proceeded to analyze Pound's work, showing his consummate literary talents and placing them ahead of any political or economic concerns which were at that time stirred up by the 1949 Bollingen controversy. Kenner took over Pound for the academics, providing exegesis, sources and context to argue for the traditions that gave his poetry both substance and currency. As the uproar over Pound's anti-Semitism, racism, Fascism and anti-capitalism slowly receded, his academic value went up.

Kenner in particular showed that *The Cantos* were not just an experiment or a set of drafts of a work in progress. He demonstrated that there was order in the work and that Pound drew from the best of historical, Oriental, classical and personal sources. Pound, some argued, had become a "contemporary *classic*" who had fashioned a modern *Divine Comedy* or *Metamorphoses* (Sullivan 202).

Following Kenner's exegesis, however, poets and the public still held Pound in abeyance, even if academia was ready to admit him. Robert Graves, the poet, represents this view. In 1955 his lecture/essay on Pound treats him with disdain, noting that to publish a poem strewn with references "to which one reader in ten million has the key" is impudent; when the author misquotes as well, the case becomes worse. Pound, "an Idaho man, left America with a patchy education," Graves continues, before recalling his introduction to him in 1922 in the rooms of T. E. Lawrence: "'Pound, Graves; Graves, Pound; you'll dislike each other'" (in Sullivan 222–3). Graves also remembered the parodies of Pound created by Gilbert Highet and Richard Aldington. Graves then castigates Pound's incomplete knowledge of Latin, Greek and Provençal. But Graves saves his harshest criticism for *The Cantos*, which he calls Pound's "sprawling, ignorant, indecent, unmelodious, seldom metrical *Cantos*, embellished with esoteric Chinese ideographs – for all I know, they may have been traced from the nearest tea-chest – and with illiterate Greek, Latin, Spanish and Provençal snippets" (in Sullivan 225).

What especially startles Graves is that the work is compulsory reading in many universities. And when a semi-lyrical passage does appear sandwiched between quotations from textbooks and "snarling polyglot parentheses," the section is usually lewd or repulsive. He quotes as an example a section from Canto L/248 beginning with

> S. .t on the throne of England, s. .t on the Austrian sofa
> In their soul was usura and in their minds darkness
> and blankness, greased fat were four Georges
> Pus was in Spain, Wellington was a jew's pimp

Graves agreed with T. E. Lawrence's assessment. Writing to his brother in 1912, Lawrence said, "Pound has a very common American affectation of immense learning in strange things," and no more (in Sullivan 226).

Donald Davie in *Ezra Pound, The Poet as Sculptor* (1964) began to effect a different view. Showing the poetic strength of Pound in a broadly based study that included Pound's Chinese translations, early poems, *Cantos* and even his translations of Sophocles, Davie challenges Graves's dismissive view. Above all, Davie celebrates Pound as a poet, beginning with the 1955 translation of *The Classic Anthology Defined by Confucius* published when Pound was sixty-nine and in St. Elizabeths. The reason? This core of Confucian ethics sums up what Pound had been striving for for over thirty years. The poems show Pound's skill with metrical variation, language and meaning and, perhaps most importantly, how Pound's engagement with genre and style necessarily pushed him to make judgments on human affairs – whether in politics, history or economics.

Davie then begins an account of Pound's life, emphasizing his preparation for a career as a literary scholar, not a poet. He then rapidly surveys Pound's early works and notes the influence of Swinburne, Morris and Rossetti, all of them out-of-step with Edwardian England. In individual works like "Piccadilly" from *Personae* (1909), Pound tips his hat toward Impressionism, inspired by John Davidson and Arthur Symons, but essentially skipped a generation as he reached back to the Victorians, a habit more characteristic of an American provincial than a British poet. Yet it would be Browning, Davie notes, who would in *Exultations* and *Personae* exert the most influence, as in "Piere Vidal Old," "Cino" and "Na Audiart." Davie skillfully shows that, in employing the dramatic monologue of Browning, Pound does something new: he modifies the form, under the influence of Provençal, into something "closer to translation or at least paraphrase," while at the same time incorporating Yeats's ideas of the "mask" to make Pound's Provençal personae less *dramatis personae* and more embodied aspects of his own personality and situation.[7]

The remainder of Davie's brisk study emphasizes the poetic context of Pound's work and its development into the full form of *The Cantos*. Meter, metaphor and melody are his concerns and Davie's own experience as a poet assists immeasurably in pinpointing Pound's talent. English poetry, as much as Pound's work, is Davie's subject, as when he outlines how, from Edmund Spenser onward, the finest art "was employed in running over the verse line so as to build up larger units of movement such as the strophe, the Miltonic verse paragraph, or, in Shakespearean and other theatrical poetry, the sustained dramatic speech" (Davie 44). One result was to submerge the pentameter "by incorporating the line into the building of larger and more intricate rhythmical units" (Davie 44).

Pound, however, reverses this in *Cathay* where the line becomes the unit of composition. Weight could now go into smaller units, but only when the line was isolated as a rhythmical unit did it become possible for the line to be rhythmically disrupted or "dismembered from within," permitting experimentation (Davie 45). Such careful attention to the poetic elements of Pound's writing and the changes he brought to the line provided new reasons to claim his importance as a major writer, while avoiding the political and economic extremes of his thought. The emphasis, Davie shows, on the component rhythmical members of a line intensifies the language of Pound's poetry, as in this line from "Song of the Bowmen of Shu" from *Cathay*:

> Horses, his horses even, are tired. They were strong.
>
> (*EPEW* 59)

Concentrating on the poetic texture of Pound's writing illuminates even the large scale. Davie's comments on "Propertius" and *Mauberley*, for example, extend his careful reading of the poetic line, noting that Pound at this stage has no intention of breaking the verse line 'but rather, in the traditional way, to submerge it by enjambment into the larger rhythmical unit of the strophe," which Davie suggests subtly registers how Pound makes his peace with Milton (Davie 90). With *Mauberley*, Davie points to the fluctuating use of tone and states that the differences in tone of voice are precisely what matter, far more than the nature of what is said. He also unexpectedly claims that Pound likely wrote *Mauberley* by ear, "by improvising and feeling forward from one poem to the next, not according to a plan" (Davie 99). Stylistically, the model was Gautier, especially in the cadence and shape of the stanzas.

Again, Davie is precise in pointing out that in *The Cantos* Pound layers one culture over another, rather than compounding or fusing distinct historical periods into some form of amalgamation. This is what Williams meant when he said Pound's object is analysis not synthesis. The breaking of the pentameter enforced the breaking down of experience into related but distinct items (Davie 123). The verse line of *The Cantos*, especially after Pound's fresh start in 1923, cracks apart, as did the Anglo-Saxon line, or the hendecasyllables of Cavalcanti. Davie summarizes this technique as the impossibility of enjambment, reinstating as the poetic unit the verse line, continually dismembered but never disintegrated (Davie 124). Davie next offers an imaginative comparison of Pound's "Malatesta Cantos" of 1923 and Williams's *In the American Grain*, his 1925 prose work, showing their similar method of telescoping and mixing history, while incorporating original documents (Davie 124–5). Pound's poem, he points out, includes a great deal of prose.

Individual chapters on individual volumes of *The Cantos* lead to Davie's offering some final comments about the poem as a whole and Pound. One of the more stimulating is that Pound succeeded in his goal of keeping the poem incomplete and baffling the critics. The poem defeats its exegetes by inviting them so inexhaustibly to examine the text; ironically, to offer an exegesis of the poem is self-defeating. The looseness of organization is deliberate, so that only through responding to its disorganized references can one appreciate the drama of the gradual drawing together of ideas in which what began as random associations arrange themselves into constellations: the rose in the steel dust as Pound imagines. This gradual clarifying occurs both in single Cantos and over a series of Cantos.

In his concluding pages, Davie takes issue with Pound's political views, believing Pound altered the role of the poet by his failure to disavow himself from the racist and extremist views he upheld. In this, Davie is like Williams, who recognized Pound's brilliance but also vilified his anti-Semitism and failure to acknowledge it (see Davie 241–2). Davie objects to any effort to disassociate the poetry from the life, and states that the effect of Pound's career negates any idea "that poetry can or should operate in the dimension of history" (Davie 244). The poet can no longer be a seer because he is too prejudiced, which invalidates *The Cantos* and Pound's vision of history. This occurred partly because history "caught up with Pound and passed him even as he wrote his poem" (Davie 245). In *The Cantos*, Pound's success with history is only elegiac, not epic. In the end, Davie sides with Williams who wrote that Pound is "one of the most competent poets in our language . . . [but] he is also, it must be confessed, the biggest damn fool and faker in the business" (in Norman 413).

Not everyone, however, read Pound or *The Cantos* so critically, indicting the work and the poet. In *The Pound Era* (1971), Hugh Kenner focused on sources and themes, pointing out where and what Pound studied, treating aesthetics, not politics. It was he who discovered that at the back of Divus's Latin translation of Homer were a set of Homeric hymns Pound used intermittently (*PE* 361). History and the historical structure of *The Cantos* are for Kenner secondary to cultural matrixes and interconnections. So the "luminous detail" on Renaissance stone pillars without annotation stand as columns to be read – and a metaphor of how to approach *The Cantos*. Pound names and we read details that show what is possible (*PE* 323, 325). Kenner points out that *arrangement* is the ultimate unit of composition, acknowledging moments of beauty among lengthy passages of what may at first glance appear to be only confusion: "under and through discrete particulars run the ordered patterns of force they delineate," he argues (*PE* 355).

The imagination in Pound's time was scaled to large works, Kenner points out, an inheritance from Shelley as much as Browning. Pound understood, however, that, for the work to be convincing, it had to link Paradise to specific historical datelines. Kenner also noted the Imagist style in moments of *The Cantos*, Imagism "a poetic of darting change" as in:

> the sea is streaked red with Adonis,
> The lights flicker red in small jars,
> Wheat shoots rise new by the altar,
> >   flower from the swift seed.
> >   (*PE* 367; XLVII/236–7)

Art "retains its own past," Kenner suggests: "forms remember." Throughout *The Cantos*, Pound displays the formal recurrences of art.

Less concerned with containing the poem in any formal sequence or shape, Kenner opens the work to its echoing polyphony of ideas and sounds – what Pound called a "horizontal chord" (in *PE* 371). By transporting simple themes to "a massive, simultaneous orchestration," Pound tried to achieve an end, incorporating not only history and economics but the entire mind of Europe. This ambition became the very stumbling block to completing the poem, according to Kenner, because Pound was working from within "a poem whose end he didn't clearly foresee," with the hope that secular events and the shape of his own life would supply a proper finale when it was time (*PE* 379). Mussolini's death, a prison cage and then twelve and a half years in a mental hospital intervened and became his story. Pound experienced the poem as he wrote it, disrupting any enforced structure or conclusion (*PE* 379). Kenner's aesthetic reading of Pound surprised many readers who had thought the work only combined the incomprehensible with the erratic.

The most challenging element of the poem became incoherence. Critics have taken an ambivalent position, recognizing Pound's refusal of closure and celebrating the openness of the work, praising its modern acknowledgment of fragmented experience at the same time they argue for a unified or at least structured form. Stephen Sicari in *Pound's Epic Ambition* (1991) reads the poem precisely in this double fashion: as a representation of disorder balanced by four complementary ideas of history that provide organization for the work. Phase one, located in the first fifty-one Cantos, is the decline of humanity from wholeness and health to pieces and enervation. Usura appears to have corrupted mankind, creating a civilization equally hostile and mean. The wanderer chooses to move away from the present in search of a lost consciousness representing a kind of home. This private journey ends with something lost but regained in Canto LXVII.

History cannot be escaped, however, and in the centrifugal movement of the work there is hope for a return to an originary consciousness. Simultaneously, then, in the first fifty-one Cantos, there is a contrary view of history. As the wanderer moved outward and away, Pound also looks at records of those people in history who worked at creating new centers via ideal states. A series of heroes appear acting for the public good and "the private vision of the wanderer-poet becomes the public goal of political action." The centrifugal movement away from the present climaxes in Canto XLVII but becomes "the centripetal reordering" around the vision of an ideal state in Canto XLIX.[8]

Pound fashioned himself the poet of the ideal Fascist state in the 1930s as part of his effort to return the world to a recoverable home. He returns to America in 1939 in the spirit of a Confucian sage but is unrecognized as such and returns to Italy and his poem. He then writes the Chinese History and Adams Cantos to provide future American leaders with a tradition of political wisdom that can restore America to its original greatness, through Jefferson and Adams, and with roots in Confucian principles. These twenty cantos (LII–LXXI) have a didactic element, copying passages from Chinese history and the Adams's papers. Recording documents now replace his quest for home, which initiates the third phase of the long poem, often considered the least poetic and most tiresome.

The fall of Mussolini required another adjustment as the ideal city faded. Pound then tried to recuperate his epic ambition which occurs in *The Pisan Cantos* when he works to convince himself and his readers of his significance in the events he identifies as history. A move from public events to private history is the new focus. His personal past and immediate present, even his body, become the center of the sequence while he remains the recorder of the dream of an ideal state which he still believes is possible. This section is both the most personal and universal as Pound purges himself of an individual identity in the midst of generating a more universal vision. This is phase three (Sicari 202).

St. Elizabeths introduces phase four where Pound must revaluate his role as an epic poet and his understanding of history, now radically represented in *Rock-Drill* and *Thrones*. He forsakes his work for an earthly paradise but one committed to history in the form of textual fragments understood as the means to a personal end. In Cantos I–LI, the personal is subordinated to the public, with a private vision the center of political action. *Rock-Drill* and *Thrones* do the reverse: the public is subordinated to the private as fragments from textual history become the material for reaching the realm of ideal justice. The goal of the poem has changed. One cannot make, but only "write Paradise" (CXVII/822). Order is possible but only through, and as, texts. A pattern of ideal justice is glimpsed but the reader must do the work of linking the fragments.

The final volume of *The Cantos, Drafts & Fragments*, evaluates his effort, acknowledging his uncertain approach to an end. Tradition, to which he calls (citing Paolo and Francesca in *Inferno* V), can ironically no longer provide a guide. Yet it is tradition that makes his articulation of loss and disorientation possible. This paradox is at the center of *The Cantos* and perhaps the modernist enterprise. There is no rest or what Pound, citing Confucius, called *chih*; only movement which destabilizes the pattern of ideal justice. But the search continues – "do not surrender perception. / And in thy mind beauty" – while the mind "unstill [is] ever turning" (CXIII/810). Pound, seventy-eight when the last Cantos were published, acknowledged the "Error of chaos" (CXIII/808) and "a tangle of works unfinished," but it does not mean the struggle to make the past usable for the present should stop (CXVI/815).

Further readers of *The Cantos* have different emphases: some see the work as a failure, underscoring Pound's Latin tag "*Litterae nihil sanantes,*" ("literature cures nothing"), a line from John Adams in a letter to Thomas Jefferson on 28 June 1812 (XXXIII/161; CXVI/815). Defeated by history, events and his own personal manias, Pound lost control of his poem, a fact which the final

Cantos confirm. The work becomes no more than a grab bag of intolerant ideas associated with anti-Semitism and Fascism. Robert Casillo provides the most extended critique of this aspect of Pound and his work.

Casillo begins *The Genealogy of Demons, Anti-Semitism, Fascism, and the Myths of Ezra Pound* (1988) with a complaint: Pound criticism has lacked objectivity. Systematic analysis of his work and ideology has not occurred. By contrast, Casillo focuses on the political, social and moral aspects of Pound's writings. What he argues is that his anti-Semitism and Fascism are systemic, inseparable "from his linguistic strategies and personal psychology."[9] Casillo then proceeds to study Pound's poetic technique and politics and finds the two united. Four stages define Pound's anti-Semitism, beginning with his suburban prejudice which shifts to a more active second phase during his 1910–11 return to America, when he discovered the extensive immigration of Jews, referring to them as "detestable" in *Patria Mia*. This continues in scattered poems and references during this period through the 1920s. Lines in "Near Perigord" where de Born tells Provençal barons they should pawn their castles to Jewish pawnbrokers and then steal them back is representative. "Let the Jews pay" is symptomatic (*EPEW* 92).

The third phase is from the late '20s to '30s, marred by Pound's increasing interest in politics and economics and a new belief that Jewish culture and religion were foreign. He also discovered usury and linked it with an international Jewish banking conspiracy, although he held back from absolute smearing. Soon, however, his literary and cultural anti-Semitism takes on a more sinister cast in his radio broadcasts and writings from the 1940s onward, the fourth phase. History, politics and culture were now to be judged in racial terms; *The Cantos* suffer: Pound blames the Jews for the American Civil War (XLVIII) and the formlessness of Middleuropa (XXXV). Canto LII denounces the Rothschilds, while Canto XCI refers to the "*kikery.*" Such language echoes some of his more virulent statements in the radio broadcasts where he declared that the Jews "infected the world," fomented chaos and were a "plague" (*EPS* 340, 320, 74).

According to Casillo, neither Pisa nor St. Elizabeths changed Pound; all America, he told Wyndham Lewis, had become the "Jewnited States" (*P/L* 291). Casillo's 463-page attack is thorough, relentlessly challenging apologists and defenders, one of his most potent charges being that critics have simply not bothered to explain the centrality of anti-Semitism in Pound's work. Despite overstatement and repetition, his study needs to be considered and evaluated.

Another contextual examination of Pound appeared the same year as Casillo's but focused on a different aspect of his career: *Stone Cottage* by James Longenbach. This examines in detail the three winters Pound and Yeats spent together in an isolated, six-room cottage on the edge of the Ashdown Forest in Sussex. Focusing on Pound's relationship with the older Yeats, Longenbach traces the exchange of ideas and techniques between the two poets: Pound becoming interested in Yeats's occult studies, Yeats beginning to write his autobiographies with Pound's assistance. Pound also read Browning's *Sordello* aloud to Yeats and began to work steadily on *The Cantos*. Both tracked the progress of the Great War and composed war poems. Importantly, Yeats introduced Pound to Joyce, while Pound presented Eliot to Yeats. Pound soon began to think of himself and Yeats as a kind of artistic elite, excluding even some of their closest friends. What Longenbach calls "the secret society of modernism" was born, an idea he develops fully in the final pages of his study. The period 1913–16 was formative not only for the work of the two writers but for the character of modernism.

In 1996, the LANGUAGE POET and critic Charles Bernstein took on the problematic issue of Pound's politics and poetry. In a provocative essay reprinted in his collection *My Way, Speeches and Poems*, Bernstein confronts the dismissal of Pound, not because of his politics but poetics – a dislike of Pound's "collage, parataxis and the very striking rhetorical surfaces of Pound's poems."[10] Criticism of Pound's Fascism, he quickly states, is *not* a move away from reading Pound or an undermining of his significance. It, rather, tries to integrate his politics and poetic practice. Bernstein's point is not to condemn or approve Pound's ideas, nor these critical approaches, but to acknowledge that the aesthetic approach (as in Kenner), part of a reaction against the post-war dismissal of Pound's writing, and the newer political approach (as in Casillo) allow for different readings of Pound's poetry.

Evaluations by the new political critics brought Bernstein back to reading Pound with the realization that his polarizing quality was exactly the reaction Pound sought. "Reading poetic forms politically" was not a bad thing. It meant "thinking through the implications of poetic structures" and realizing that they can never be neutral or transparent (*MW* 156–7). Importantly, Bernstein acknowledges that a poem including history means one must pay attention to that history which is "writ in the style, in the symbolic/semiotic economy of the poem, in the material means of production" as much as in Pound's ideas (*MW* 157). Poetry is not worth reading, he announces, "because it is comfortable or happy or understandable or uplifting any more than history or philosophy is" (*MW* 157).

Bernstein admits that Pound was delusional, especially during the period of the Rome radio broadcasts. But Pound had different politics and poetics at different times in his life. He was inconsistent, at one period in the thirties maintaining a dialogue with the political left. But Pound's poetry is never just a reflection of his politics and Bernstein offers a counterview: that Pound's poetry contradicts his Fascism, although he does not fully explain how and calls Pound's anti-Semitism something "not related to his hatred of individual Jews." Pound's view of Jews is "highly theoretical and structural, projecting Jewishness, more than individual Jews" (*MW* 158). Bernstein understands this demonizing as part of Pound's "systematic paranoia-producing ideology" (*MW* 158). Yet Pound's work provokes an ideological reading, Bernstein admits, insisting, in fact, that it be read for its politics and ideas, two of its enduring values. Pound's dystopian elements need to be explored as much as his lyrical. His political "disease" is part of his poetic "health," Bernstein suggests (*MW* 159).

"The irresolvability of the problem is Pound's legacy," Bernstein writes in a companion piece, a revision of a 1985 talk he gave at a Pound conference at Yale (*MW* 160). The Fascist roots of Pound's innovations in *The Cantos* are unavoidable, he believes. He then specifically turns to Pound's use of montage and collage to identify the Fascist implications of these techniques in his work, to show how the text implodes the very objectivity it purports to express in its use of extra-literary materials. Bernstein also introduces the idea of a compositional field in the work, field poetry if you will, the result of Pound creating a multiple set of sometimes contradictory and competitive voices in his poem, with the corresponding absence of a fulcrum or point of arbitration, except that of the reader. Listening, not judging, might describe the situation, where no one person has the knowledge or vantage point to make it whole – the point of the poem, but one that Pound was himself reluctant to accept (*MW* 161).

Another recent reading of Pound's work focuses on the material aspect of his modernism. This centers on the cultural influence of modernism and recognizes its institutional features, from its elitism to its hostility to mass culture. The complexities of cultural exchange and circulation, however, revise this opposition and demonstrate new orders of relations. The commodification of modernism is one expression of this union, a subject Lawrence Rainey has explored in *Institutions of Modernism* (1998). Of particular note is attention to the deluxe editions of Pound's work, examined by Jerome McGann and George Bornstein. This examination of material modernism underscores the way Pound's poems first appeared and the kind of audience he imagined, one that could appreciate the physical art, if not the poetry, of *A Draft of XVI Cantos*, for example, and pay attention to the unique publishing features of each volume, printed by small presses in limited runs in Paris or London.

Textual studies preceded this new interest in the physical book. This principally took the form of attempting to establish a consistent and textually reliable edition of *The Cantos*. From the effort to produce a variorum edition of the poem, initiated by Richard Taylor, to Peter Stoicheff's detailed study of the endings of the poem and Christine Froula's study of errors in the work, textual studies has made important contributions to understanding Pound's work. Froula, interestingly, expands the idea of error to contextualizing elements of erroneous history in the poem. Initially, she means Pound's inclusion of printers' errors, mis-attributions, mis-translations and other problems in the text of *The Cantos*, which corrupt its history. But error also suggests errantry or wandering away from fact, a move Pound often repeats.

But there still remains the question of Pound's relation to modernism, which Peter Nicholls, in "Modernising Modernism: from Pound to Oppen,"[11] among others, begins to re-evaluate. Essentially this is a critique of Pound's refusal to recognize how violence surpassed reason in the twentieth century. The brutal facts of Europe's political disaster and moral horror brought about by the Second World War have been put before Pound and he has been found inadequate. Pound's blindness to the effects of the war in his long poem restrict his acceptance or at least complicate it. One reading of Pound's refusal to reason, rejecting logical, syntactic propositions, is to understand his paratactic structures as an irrational response to the modern age, response without comment. The ideological implications question the sincerity of Pound's late project. Doing may not always be better than thinking.

Marjorie Perloff's 2004 essay "Pound Ascendant" continues the critique,[12] addressing the disparity between Pound's advanced criticism and his poetry, which for the most part does not follow the objective method. Rather, she shows in detail how Pound reverts back almost to an Elizabethan diction, especially when dealing with the mythical and allusive. Pound's poetic language, she argues, is detached from everyday practice and contradicts his maxims and theorems of poetic use.

Nevertheless, the advanced technique of *The Cantos*, relying on a fusion of the ideogram, document, myth and citation, helps to define its uniqueness. The frequent use of "collage cuts" that startle and quickly jump from the autobiographical/memoir are further aspects of originality in the remarkable *Pisan Cantos*, recalling, from moment to moment, Yeats or Joyce or restaurants in Clinton, New York (the home of Hamilton College) or the most elusive classical myths.[13] But despite the contradictions between his poetic theory and practice, Pound, Perloff concludes, cannot be overlooked. As she asks, "What other 20th-century poet has had so ambitious a project?"

The estrangement of language from current linguistic norms nonetheless relates Pound to such later phenomena as the "mongrelisme" of LANGUAGE POETS like Joan Retallack and the homophonic translations of Steve McCaffery or Charles Bernstein. Jackson Mac Low's 1983 poem, published in 1989 and entitled *Words nd Ends from Ez*, demonstrates the innovative, open, almost investigative poetry resulting from Pound's efforts. This poetry rejects received notions of unity, closure and prosody. The work selects chance words and fragments from *The Cantos*, based on the positioning of the letters in E-Z-R-A P-O-U-N-D. A sample:

> oZier's curve he wAll,
> Phin hOut exUltant
> seeN impiDity,
> Exultance,
> aZ loRr-
> leAf
> Paler rOck-
> layers at-
> *Un* e deNho ia

The first line is derived from "The crozier's curve runs in the wall," the second line of Canto CX. The Z is in the second-letter position (eZra), the R in the third-letter position (ezRa) (in *MW* 164).

Pound's influence on 21st-century poetry remains, although a question persists: how harmful were his obsessions and manias? How did they affect his poetry and reputation? But this may be the wrong, or at least not the only, question to ask and avoids looking directly at either his achievements or defeats. The answer may be to adopt the paratactic strategy of Pound himself before drawing any conclusions. A "monolinear syllogistic" answer may be too narrow and should be replaced by the Poundian method of "examining a dozen or two dozen facts and putting them all together" (*J/M* 28). To discredit Pound's poetics *tout court* because of his Fascist allegiances may be too simple a process; it is certainly too easy.

Pound's influence is for many unquestionable, even if his politics remain repugnant and his reputation controversial. American contemporaries like Robert Lowell, Charles Olson, Robert Creeley, Randall Jarrell, Allen Ginsberg, Robert Duncan and Donald Hall acknowledge his stature. Edwin Morgan, Donald Davie, Charles Tomlinson, Thom Gunn, Geoffrey Hill and Roy Fisher are among British poets most influenced by his work. Marjorie Perloff broadly positioned Pound when she asked, "what poet writing in England or America since World War II has *not* learned from Pound?" (*COG* 196). Lorine Niedecker, James Merrill, Denise Levertov, Paul Blackburn and the LANGUAGE POETS Charles Bernstein and Jackson Mac Low are among younger writers who have acknowledged Pound's presence in shaping their work. Only partly in jest, Laughlin expressed Pound's importance when he addressed a 1947 letter to him with the heading, "METRICAL MONARCH" (*EP/JL* 165).

Pound, himself, was hesitant to make any claims of influence on younger poets. When the American poet Jack Gilbert visited Pound in Merano in 1960 and asked him if he thought newer poets would continue to write in the tradition of *The Cantos*, Pound sat silent. After twenty minutes, he said "No, what I have done for the young poets is to make it possible for them to put things in their poems."[14] *The Cantos* became an encyclopedia of possibilities.

Pound's poetic, Marjorie Perloff claims, "has become synonymous with modernism itself" (*COG* 197). Declarations such as "use no superfluous word, no adjective which does not reveal something" or "Go in fear of abstractions" (*LE* 4–5) now seem axiomatic. The focus on the particular, the object, is the core of modernist poetry, a rallying cry for poets as diverse as the Objectivist George Oppen or the modernist Frank O'Hara. Basil Bunting understood the importance of this principle well, telling Louis Zukofsky in 1932 that Pound had developed "a pervading stress on the immediate . . . shrinking from even the suspicion of verbalism." His poetics "will build with facts but declines to soar with inevitably unsteady words." *The Cantos* contain, as Ginsberg told Pound, "practical exact language models which are scattered through *The Cantos* like stepping stones."[15] Pound writes of the things seen, in the past as well as the present.

New editions of Pound's letters continue to contribute to his re-evaluation. One of the most important is Ezra and Dorothy Pound, *Letters in Captivity 1945–1946*, edited by Omar Pound and Robert Spoo (1999). This consists of correspondence written from the time of his first arrest and interrogation by the US Army at the Counter Intelligence Headquarters in Genoa through the Pisa period to St. Elizabeths, ending with Dorothy's first visit to him in Washington in July 1946. New editions of Pound's own work have also been appearing, notably *A Walking Tour in Southern France* (1992) and the prose essays collected in *Machine Art & Other Writings, The Lost Thought of the Italian Years* (1996). Academic articles and monographs that focus on his poetic language, translations and Italian experience continue to be published.

Pound's life also maintains its fascination. Ever since Humphrey Carpenter's massive, 1,005-page biography (1988), reviews of Pound's life have been appearing, including Anne Conover's *Olga Rudge and Ezra Pound* (2001) and Ira B. Nadel's briefer *Ezra Pound, A Literary Life* (2004). Two new "lives" are expected in the next several years, one a two-volume biography, the other a detailed account digging deeply into American and Italian sources. A new helpful source is an autobiography by Pound's father, Homer (written 1929, published 2003). Entitled *Small Boy*, it reveals a great deal about the Pound family history. Two additional and recent reference works are *The Cambridge Companion to Ezra*

Pound (1999) and the more recent *Ezra Pound Encyclopedia* (2005). Biblio-graphical work is also ongoing, with updates of Donald Gallup's magisterial work, *Ezra Pound A Bibliography* (2nd edn. 1983), regularly appearing.

Other new areas of Pound's work receiving attention include his role as an anthologist, and his study of the visual arts and use of radio, as noted in Margaret Fisher's *Ezra Pound's Radio Operas* (2002). Contextual studies of his poetry – whether within the Vorticist tradition, modernism or Confucianism – now appear with regularity. Several recent titles are Catherine E. Paul's *Poetry in the Museums of Modernism, Yeats, Pound, Moore, Stein* (2002), Miranda Hickman's *The Geometry of Modernism, The Vorticist Idiom in Lewis, Pound, H. D. and Yeats* (2005) and Feng Lan's *Ezra Pound and Confucianism, Remaking Humanism in the Face of Modernity* (2005). Two recent collections marking additional directions are *Ezra Pound and African American Modernism*, ed. Michael Coyle (2001) and *Ezra Pound and China*, ed. Zhaoming Qian (2003).

New textual editions of Pound's poetry are also appearing, although plans for a variorum edition of *The Cantos* are on hold. Massimo Bacigalupo, however, has edited and published *Canti Postumi* (2002), a comprehensive selection of deletions, rewrites and cancelled passages from *The Cantos*. This bilingual (English–Italian) edition supplements the full edition of the poem edited by Mary de Rachewiltz, *I Cantos*, published by Modadori in 1985. One of the most important critical editions now available, however, is *The Pisan Cantos*, ed. Richard Sieburth (2003) with full and useful notes and, most helpfully, line numbers, the first extended Pound text to include them.

Pound's *Poems and Translations* (2003), also edited by Sieburth, is the fullest one-volume collection of his work currently available and includes the *Sonnets and Ballate of Cavalcanti, 'Noh' or Accomplishment, Confucius: The Great Digest and The Wobbling Pivot, The Confucian Analects, The Classic Anthology Defined by Confucius* and *Sophocles: The Women of Trachis*. It also publishes his satirical poem "Redondillas, or Something of That Sort," which opens in a mock heroic style with "I sing the gaudy to-day and cosmopolite civiliza-tion" (*EPPT* 175) but which was removed at the last moment from the proofs of *Canzoni*. Sieburth's volume appears in the important Library of America series, a sign of Pound's acceptance into the canon of modern American liter-ature. A shorter, paperback collection of Pound's work, *Early Writings, Poems and Prose* (2005), includes Fenollosa's influential prose work edited by Pound, "The Chinese Written Character as a Medium for Poetry."

"I don't so much write as roar," Pound told his publisher James Laughlin (*EP/JL* 132). In many ways this sums up his energy, intent and determina-tion to manage, if not produce, many of the key figures in the establishment of modernism. He also constantly fought for clarity, although he often had difficulty in achieving it in his own poetry. As he explained in a letter, "there is *no intentional* obscurity. There is condensation to maximum attainable" (*SL* 322–3). His interests were many, his actions diverse, his social ideas intemperate. His politics and economics distorted his thinking with serious consequences, affecting his poetry, criticism and reception. Yet his writing is always instructive, Charles Olson offering a clear statement of Pound's value in his manifesto, "Projective Verse." There, he notes that the syllable is "the king and pin of versification," but that it had been lost until Pound restored it (in Davie 246). For this reconstruction of the verse line as the unit of composition, American and English poets must be grateful.

"I have no life / save when the swords clash" seems to epitomize Pound, the line taken from his early poem "Sestina Altaforte." Pound's impatient, moralizing voice, castigating, charging and threatening (he actually fenced in university and once challenged a London critic to a duel over Milton, although some say it was Wordsworth), sought to lead many out of a cultural wilderness, preceded by a phalanx of banners blowing gallantly in the wind. Upon them, sayings both pithy and extreme:

> Literature is news that STAYS news   (*ABCR* 29)
>
> History without monetary intelligence is mere twaddle   (*SL* 336)
>
> Critics should know more and write less   (*SP* 359)
>
> The supreme crime in a critic is dullness   (*GK* 161)

Pound was intense; each sentence for him was an idea (*CC* 333). But he never questioned the moral value of literature. Its purpose was ethical, functioning in the state to demonstrate the "clarity and vigour" of thought and opinion (*LE* 21). Literature keeps language clear, but when language goes rotten, so, too, does civic and individual thought (*LE* 21). Coupled with his certainty was an unstoppable energy, characterized by Wyndham Lewis when he called Pound the "demon pantechnicon driver, busy with removal of the old world into new quarters" (*CRH* 116). Pound was always supercharged.

Pound had a mission expressed through the Confucian goals of clear thought and ethical action, but, at times, he did not recognize the path and stood in confusion, which he admitted in a late canto: "I lost my center / fighting the world" (CXVII/822). But he always understood what poetry must do: guide the culture, maintain clarity and sustain "thousands of active words" (EPEW 325). William Carlos Williams, and others, knew that Pound was "possessed of the most acute ear for metrical sequences, to the point of genius, that we have ever known" (in Sullivan 203), while Eliot recognized that "artistic creation is always a complicated turning inside out of old forms" – exactly what Pound did through his cajoling, badgering and impressive ways.[16]

Pound was a quintessential modernist, a figure who blithely but knowledge-ably overturned poetic meter, literary style and the state of the long poem. Only his experimentation with new forms and determination to "make it new" exceeded his boldness in editing *The Waste Land*, resolve in publishing *Ulysses*, and originality in beginning new movements like Imagism. "I do not teach," he wrote in a note to his early poem "Histrion," "I awake." To William Carlos Williams, he was

> a man
> whose words will
>   bite
>   their way
> home – being actual
> having the form
>   of motion[17]

To readers, he was a constant challenge: "Explode: let's hear what you have and what you think" (*SL* 183).

Notes

1 Life

1. Pound in Charles Norman, *Ezra Pound*. Rev. edn. (London: Macmillan, 1969) 5. Hereafter cited as "Norman."
2. Yeats in Patricia Hutchins, *Ezra Pound's Kensington, An Exploration 1885–1913* (Chicago: Henry Regnery Company, 1965) 85.
3. Pound in Michael Reck, *Ezra Pound, A Close-Up* (New York. McGraw-Hill, 1967) 986.
4. Yeats in A. Norman Jeffares, *W. B. Yeats, Man and Poet* (London: Routledge & Kegan Paul, 1949) 167.
5. Pound in K. K. Ruthven, *Ezra Pound as Literary Critic* (London: Routledge, 1990) 141.
6. Aldington in Charles Doyle, *Richard Aldington, A Biography* (London: Macmillan, 1989) 87–8.

2 Context

1. Douglas Golding, *South Lodge* (London: Constable, 1943) 40. Also see Lucy McDiarmid, "A Box for Wilfrid Blunt," *PMLA* 120 (January 2005): 163–80. Hereafter "McDiarmid."
2. Yeats in Richard Aldington, "Presentation to Mr. W. S. Blunt," *The Egoist* (2 February 1914): 56.
3. Virginia Woolf, "Mr. Bennett and Mrs. Brown," *Collected Essays*, ed. Leonard Woolf, vol. I (London: Chatto and Windus, 1968) 320; *The Diary of Virginia Woolf*, vol. II, *1920–4*. ed. Anne Oliver Bell (Harmondsworth: Penguin, 1978) 223–4.
4. T. S. Eliot, "Ulysses, Order and Myth," *James Joyce, Two Decades of Criticism*, ed. Sion Givens (New York: Vanguard Press, 1963) 201.
5. Pierre Lalo, *Le Temps* (Paris, June 1913) n.p.
6. Solomon Eagle [i.e., J. C. Squire] "Current Literature: Books in General," *New Statesman* 3.65 (4 July 1914): 406.
7. W. B. Yeats, "Certain Noble Plays of Japan," *Essays and Introductions* (London: Macmillan, 1961) 230–1.
8. Wyndham Lewis, *Blasting and Bombardiering* (London: Calder, 1982) 250, 15.

9. T. E. Hulme, "Romanticism and Classicism," *Speculations*, ed. Herbert Read (London: Routledge and Kegan Paul, 1936) 126–7, 132.

10. Reed Way Dasenbrock, *Imitating the Italians* (Baltimore: Johns Hopkins University Press, 1991) 114.

11. For an account of Pound's Latin studies see Ron Thomas, *The Latin Masks of Ezra Pound* (Ann Arbor: UMI Research Press, 1983) 165. Additional studies of Pound and the classics include Peter Davidson, *Ezra Pound and Roman Poetry* (Amsterdam: Rodopi, 1995); Lillian Feder, "Pound and Ovid," *Ezra Pound Among the Poets*, ed. George Bornstein (Chicago: University of Chicago Press, 1985) 13–34; Daniel M. Hooley, *The Classics in Paraphrase, Ezra Pound and Modern Translators of Latin Poetry* (London: Associated University Presses, 1988); J. P. Sullivan, *Ezra Pound and Sextus Propertius, A Study in Creative Translation* (London: Faber and Faber, 1965); and Sullivan's "Ezra Pound and the Classics," *New Approaches to Ezra Pound*, ed. Eva Hesse (London: Faber and Faber, 1969) 215–41.

12. See Feng Lau, *Ezra Pound and Confucianism, Remaking Humanism in the Face of Modernity* (Toronto: University of Toronto Press, 2005) 14–32, and Norman J. Girardot, *The Victorian Translation of China, James Legge's Oriental Pilgrimage* (Berkeley: University of California Press, 2002). This last is both a biography and a nuanced cultural history, which points out, for example, that Legge's earliest lectures at Oxford (November–December 1876) were titled "Nature and History of Chinese Written Characters" (Girardot, 539). Pound refers to Legge in LXXX/514.

3 Works

1. Outerbridge in Sarah Milroy, "Maggs, a Life in Two Parts," *Globe and Mail* (15 March 2006): R 1.

2. Pound in Hugh Witemeyer, *The Poetry of Ezra Pound, Forms and Renewal 1908–1920* (Berkeley: University of California Press, 1981) 119. Hereafter "Witemeyer."

3. In Peter Brooker, *Bohemia in London, The Social Scene of Early Modernism* (Basingstoke: Palgrave/Macmillan, 2004) 98. Also see pp. 114–23 on Vorticist dinners.

4. Donald Davie, *Ezra Pound, Poet as Sculptor* (New York: Oxford University Press, 1964) 44–5. Hereafter "Davie."

5. Marjorie Perloff, "The Contemporary of Our Grandchildren, Pound's Influence," *Ezra Pound Among the Poets*, ed. George Bornstein (Chicago: University of Chicago Press, 1985) 203. Hereafter "*COG*."

6. Pound in K. K. Ruthven, *A Guide to Ezra Pound's Personae (1926)* (Berkeley: University of California Press, 1969) 127.

7. John Espey, *Ezra Pound's Mauberley, A Study in Composition.* (Berkeley: University of California Press, 1974) 14. Hereafter "Espey."

8. Ian F. A. Bell, "The Middle Cantos XLII–LXXI," *The Cambridge Companion to Ezra Pound*, ed. Ira B. Nadel (Cambridge: Cambridge University Press, 1999) 105.

9. For a translation of both Cantos, see Massimo Bacigalupo, "Ezra Pound's Cantos 72 and 73: An Annotated Translation," *Paideuma* 20 (1991): 11–41. Parts of LXXII and all of LXXIII appeared in the paper *La Marina Repubblicana* in January and February 1945.

10. Pound in Donald Hall, "Ezra Pound," *Writers at Work, The Paris Review Interviews,* 2nd series, ed. Malcolm Cowley (New York: Viking, 1963) 58.

11. Michael Alexander, *The Poetic Achievement of Ezra Pound* (Berkeley: University of California Press, 1979) 43.

12. Wyndham Lewis, "Plain Home-Builder: Where is Your Vorticist?" *Wyndham Lewis on Art,* ed. Walter Michel and C. J. Fox. (New York: Funk and Wagnalls, 1969) 278. On Pound's turn to Fascism, see Lawrence Rainey, "From the Patron to *il Duce*: Ezra Pound's Odyssey," *Institutions of Modernism* (New Haven: Yale University Press, 1998) Ch.4 and Tim Redman, "The Turn to Fascism," *Ezra Pound and Italian Fascism* (Cambridge: Cambridge University Press, 1991) Ch. 4.

13. Samuel Beckett, "Ex Cathezra," *Disjecta* (New York: Grove Press 1984) 79.

14. Mina Loy, "Feminist Manifesto," *The Lost Lunar Baedeker: Poems of Mina Loy* , ed. Roger L. Conover (Manchester: Carcanet, 1997) 153.

15. Basil Bunting to Pound in Peter Makin, *Bunting: The Shaping of His Verse* (Oxford: Clarendon Press, 1992) 79; *EP/JL* 109.

16. This was the version which appeared in the first edition of BLAST (20 June 1914). Pound altered the language when he reprinted it in *Personae* (1926) to read "Let us be done with pandars and jobbery, / Let us spit upon those who pat the big-bellies for profit" (*EPPT* 569).

17. Ezra Pound to Allen Ginsberg in "Encounters with Ezra Pound," *City Lights Anthology,* ed. Lawrence Ferlinghetti (San Francisco: City Lights, 1974) 13–15. Hereafter "Ginsberg."

18. On Pound, the modernists and anti-Semitism, see Robert Casillo, *The Genealogy of Demons: Anti-Semitism, Fascism and the Myths of Ezra Pound* (Evanston: Northwestern University Press, 1988), which argues that the ideology of Fascism and Pound's poetry, including his anti-Semitism, are united; Anthony Julius, *T. S. Eliot, Anti-Semitism and Literary Form* (Cambridge: Cambridge University Press, 1995), a careful analysis of anti-Semitism in his work; and Leon Surette, *Pound in Purgatory, From Economic Radicalism to Anti-Semitism* (Urbana: University of Illinois Press, 1999), which examines Pound's economic journalism and the links between his ideas on economics, Fascism and racism.

19. Dante, "Inferno, Canto XXXIII," *The Divine Comedy,* tr. Allen Mandelbaum (London: Everyman, 1995) 204.

4 Critical reception

1. Ernest Hemingway, *A Moveable Feast* (New York: Charles Scribner's Sons, 1964) *Ezra Pound, A Critical Anthology,* ed. J. P. Sullivan (Harmondsworth: Penguin, 1970) 184. Hereafter "Sullivan"; 110; W. B. Yeats on Pound in e. e. cummings in Jesse Rosse,

EP in His Time and Beyond (Newark, DE: University of Delaware Library, 2006) 17; T. S. Eliot, Dedication, to "The Waste Land," *Poems 1909–1925* (London: Faber & Gwyer, 1925). Pound had used the phrase as the title of his chapter on Arnaut Daniel in *The Spirit of Romance.*

2. W. B. Yeats, "Preface," *Oxford Book of Modern Verse 1892–1935*, ed. W. B. Yeats (Oxford: Clarendon Press, 1936) xxiv–xxvi; Geoffrey Grigson, "The Methodism of Ezra Pound," *New Verse* 5 (October 1933), rptd. in *CRH* 259–64; William Carlos Williams, "Excerpts from a Critical Sketch: *A Draft of XXX Cantos* by Ezra Pound," *Selected Essays* (New York: Random House, 1954) 107. Hereafter "Williams."

3. Louis Zukofsky, "Ezra Pound," *Prepositions, The Collected Critical Essays of Louis Zukofsky* (New York: Horizon Press, 1968) 61. Hereafter "Zukofsky."

4. Williams, 111.

5. Ronald Bottrall, "XXX Cantos of Ezra Pound: An Incursion into Poetics," in Sullivan, 135.

6. Marianne Moore in Peter Wilson, *A Preface to Ezra Pound* (London: Longman, 1997) 176.

7. Donald Davie, *Ezra Pound, The Poet as Sculptor* [1964] (New York: Oxford University Press, 1968) 23. Hereafter "Davie."

8. Stephen Sicari, *Pound's Epic Ambition, Dante and The Modern World* (Albany: State University of New York Press, 1991) 200. Hereafter "Sicari."

9. Robert Casillo, *The Genealogy of Demons, Anti-Semitism, Fascism, and the Myths of Ezra Pound* (Evanston, IL: Northwestern University Press, 1988) viii. Hereafter "Casillo."

10. Charles Bernstein "Pound and the Poetry of Today," *My Way, Speeches and Poems* (Chicago: University of Chicago Press, 1999) 156. Hereafter "*MW.*"

11. *Critical Inquiry* 44 (2002): 41–58.

12. *Boston Poetry Review* (April–May 2004).

13. Perloff, "Pound Ascendant," *Boston Poetry Review* 52–4.

14. Jack Gilbert, "The Craft of the Invisible," *Ironwood* 24 (Fall 1984): 156.

15. Basil Bunting, "Open Letter to Louis Zukofsky," *Basil Bunting, Man and Poet*, ed. Carroll F. Terrell (Orono, ME: National Poetry Foundation, 1980) 242; Allen Ginsberg, "Encounters with Ezra Pound, Journal Notes," *City Lights Anthology* (1974), rptd. in *Composed on the Tongue* (Bolinas: Grey Fox Press, 1980) 4–5.

16. T. S. Eliot, *The Use of Poetry and The Use of Criticism* (London: Faber, 1964) 135.

17. William Carlos Williams, "The Wind," *Collected Poems*, ed. A. Walton Litz and Christopher MacGowan, vol. I (New York: New Directions, 1986) 339.

Guide to further reading

Life

Carpenter, Humphrey. *A Serious Character, The Life of Ezra Pound*. London: Faber and Faber, 1988. An extensive and lengthy account of the poet.

Conover, Anne. *Olga Rudge and Ezra Pound*. New Haven: Yale University Press, 2001. A biography of the Olga Rudge / Ezra Pound relationship spanning nearly fifty years.

Cornell, Julian. *The Trial of Ezra Pound*. New York: John Day, 1966. An account by Pound's lawyer of his days in and out of court.

Nadel, Ira B. *Ezra Pound, A Literary Life*. Houndmills, Basingstoke: Palgrave/Macmillan, 2004. A short life centering on Pound the poet and critic.

Stock, Noel. *Life of Ezra Pound*. 2nd edn. San Francisco: North Point Press, 1982. A useful early narrative written with Pound's support.

Torrey, E. Fuller. *The Roots of Treason: Ezra Pound and the Secret of St. Elizabeths*. New York: McGraw-Hill, 1984. A spirited account of Pound's life at St. Elizabeths.

Wilhelm, James. *The American Roots of Ezra Pound*. New York: Garland, 1985. Details of Pound's early American experiences.

Contexts

Barnhisel, Gregory. *James Laughlin, New Directions and The Remaking of Ezra Pound*. Amherst, MA: University of Massachusetts Press, 2005. An important study of Pound and his publisher.

Brooker, Peter. *Bohemia in London, The Social Scene of Early Modernism*. Houndmills, Basingstoke: Palgrave–Macmillan, 2004. Pound as a player in London's literary and bohemian life.

Hickman, Miranda. *The Geometry of Modernism, The Vorticist Idiom in Lewis, Pound, H. D. and Yeats*. Austin: University of Texas Press, 2005. Useful contextualization of Vorticism in the development of modernism, uniting literature and the visual arts, focusing on the idiom and metaphors of geometric forms.

Kenner, Hugh. *The Pound Era*. Berkeley: University of California Press, 1971. A fundamental assessment of Pound's work and importance in shaping the modernist tradition. Still the most inventive book on Pound.

Longenbach, James. *Stone Cottage, Pound, Yeats and Modernism*. New York: Oxford University Press, 1988. An important account of the shaping poetic practices of Pound, Yeats and the modernists.

Works

Bacigalupo, Massimo. *The Forméd Trace: The Later Poetry of Ezra Pound*. New York: Columbia University Press, 1980. A full discussion of the development of Pound's late work.

Bush, Ronald. *The Genesis of Ezra Pound's Cantos*. [1976.] Princeton: Princeton University Press, 1989. A solid textual study of the evolution of the poem.

Dasenbrock, Reed Way. *Imitating the Italians: Wyatt, Spenser, Synge, Pound, Joyce.* Baltimore: Johns Hopkins University Press, 1991. The Italian and English poetic context for Pound's writing.

[Eliot, T. S.]. "Ezra Pound: His Metric and Poetry," *To Criticize the Critic and Other Writings*. [1917.] New York: Farrar Straus & Giroux, 1965. 162–82. An important early analysis of Pound's writing.

Espey, John. *Ezra Pound's Mauberley, A Study in Composition*. Berkeley: University of California Press, 1974. A detailed reading of the poem.

Froula, Christine. *To Write Paradise: Style and Authority in Pound's Cantos*. New Haven: Yale University Press, 1984. An important engagement with Pound's use of error and the question of authority in Pound's long poem.

Gallup, Donald. *Ezra Pound: A Bibliography*. 2nd ed. Charlottesville: University Press of Virginia, 1983. A complete bibliography of Pound's publications, although supplements by diverse hands have appeared since this edition. Essential.

Hutchins, Patricia. *Ezra Pound's Kensington*. Chicago: Henry Regnery Company, 1965. Useful description of Pound's early London life.

Kenner, Hugh. *The Poetry of Ezra Pound*. [1951.] Lincoln: University of Nebraska Press, 1985. The first extended reading of Pound's poetry, superseded only by Kenner's *The Pound Era* (1971) which contextualizes Pound's work in the broad frame of modernism.

Pound, Ezra. *Canti postumi*. Ed. Massimo Bacigalupo. Rome: Mondadori, 2002. A dual-language edition of cancelled and revised Cantos.

The Cantos. New York: New Directions, 1995. Thirteenth printing which includes Cantos LXXII and LXXIII, the Italian Cantos.

Early Writings, Poems and Prose. Ed. Ira B Nadel. New York: Penguin, 2005. A representative collection of poetry and prose, including Fenollosa's "The Chinese Written Character as a Medium for Poetry."

"Ezra Pound Speaking." Radio Speeches of World War II. Ed. Leonard W. Doob. Westport, CT: Greenwood Press, 1978. The only accessible edition of the radio speeches.

Literary Essays. Ed. T. S. Eliot. [1954.] New York: New Directions, 1968. Essential Pound.

The Pisan Cantos. Ed. Richard Sieburth. New York: New Directions, 2003. The best edited text of this section of the poem. Useful introduction and notes.

Poems and Translations. Ed. Richard Sieburth. New York: Library of America, 2003. Most comprehensive one-volume collection of Pound's poetry now available.

Poetry and Prose, Contributions to Periodicals. 11 vols. Ed. Lea Baechler, A. Walton Litz and James Longenbach. New York: Garland, 1991. Facsimiles of Pound's original contributions. Important.

Selected Prose 1909–1965. Ed. William Cookson. London: Faber and Faber, 1973. An important collection of Pound's writing with sections on money, poetry and contemporaries. Includes his "Treatise on Harmony."

Pound, Homer. *A Small Boy: The Wisconsin Childhood of Homer L. Pound.* Ed. Alec Marsh. Hailey, ID: Ezra Pound Association, 2003. A revealing document.

Rainey, Lawrence S. *Ezra Pound and the Monument of Culture: Text, History and the Malatesta Cantos.* Chicago: University of Chicago Press, 1991. The most detailed account yet published of Pound's research and writing the Malatesta Cantos.

Ruthven, K. K. *A Guide to Ezra Pound's Personae (1926).* Berkeley: University of California Press, 1969. A useful guide to the many poems in Pound's text.

Terrell, Carroll F. *A Companion to the Cantos of Ezra Pound.* 2 vols. Berkeley: University of California Press, 1980. An essential source for references and allusions to *The Cantos.*

Witemeyer, Hugh. *The Poetry of Ezra Pound, Forms and Renewal 1908–1920.* [1969.] Berkeley: University of California Press, 1981. An important survey of Pound's early poetic writings.

Yeats, W. B. *Letters of William Butler Yeats.* Ed. Alan Wade. London: Rupert Hart-Davis, 1954. A useful guide to the Yeats–Pound association and Yeats' own poetic practice.

Critical reception

Alexander, Michael, and James McGonigal, eds. *Sons of Ezra: British Poets and Ezra Pound.* Amsterdam: Rodopi, 1995. A collection on Ezra Pound's influence on modern British poets.

Casillo, Robert. *The Genealogy of Demons: Anti-Semitism, Fascism, and the Myths of Ezra Pound.* Evanston, IL: Northwestern University Press, 1988. A lengthy analysis of the anti-Semitism and Fascism in Pound's work.

Ezra Pound, The Critical Heritage. Ed. Eric Homberger London: Routledge & Kegan Paul, 1972. An important collection of contemporary critical commentary on Pound's works, organized by individual titles.

The Ezra Pound Encyclopedia. ed. Demetres P. Tryphonopoulos and Stephen J. Adams. Westport, CT: Greenwood, Press, 2005. A useful encyclopedia of Pound's terms, texts, ideas and people.

Nadel, Ira B., ed. *The Cambridge Companion to Ezra Pound.* Cambridge: Cambridge University Press, 1999. Fifteen essays that cover the poetry and prose of Pound, including his work as critic, translator, composer, economics writer and editor.

Paideuma. 1972. A journal founded for scholarship and criticism on Ezra Pound, since 2002 expanded to include American and British modernist poetry. Published by the National Poetry Foundation at the University of Maine, Orono, Maine.

Perloff, Marjorie. "Pound Ascendant," *Boston Review* April–May 2004. www.bostonreview.net/BR29.2/perloff.html. An important recent assessment.

"Pound/Stevens: Whose Era?" *The Dance of the Intellect: Studies in the Poetry of the Pound Tradition.* Cambridge: Cambridge University Press, 1985. 1–32. A stimulating and important encounter with the Pound tradition challenged by Wallace Stevens.

Rainey, Lawrence. *Institutions of Modernism: Literary Elites and Public Culture.* New Haven: Yale University Press, 1998. An important discussion of the market capital of modernism. See esp. ch. 4, "From the Patron to *il Duce*: Ezra Pound's Odyssey."

Redman, Timothy. *Ezra Pound and Italian Fascism.* Cambridge: Cambridge University Press, 1991. A detailed examination using many original sources for Pound's economic and Fascist beliefs.

Stoicheff, Peter. *The Hall of Mirrors: Drafts & Fragments and the End of Ezra Pound's Cantos.* Ann Arbor: University of Michigan Press, 1995. An in-depth analysis of Pound's problems with completing *The Cantos*.

Index